THE VIEW FROM LENIN HILLS

THE VIEW FROM LENIN HILLS

Soviet Youth in Ferment

WILLIAM TAUBMAN

COWARD-McCANN, Inc.

NEW YORK

Library of Congress Catalog Card Number: 67-23145

Printed in the United States of America
By American Book–Stratford Press, Inc.

Contents

1

The Man from the Central Committee

"I WANT TO SPEAK with you tonight frankly and objectively about whatever is on your mind."

The speaker was a member and staff official of the Central Committee of the Communist Party of the Soviet Union. His listeners were Moscow State University students.

"Would you like to fire questions at me immediately?" The speaker glanced quickly around the crowded duplex lounge that serves the seventeenth and eighteenth floors of the university dormitory. "Or would you prefer me to say a few words first?"

"Let's hear you for a while," shouted someone in the rear whom I couldn't see. The demand sounded rude and irreverent to me. Could it be that students would dare to pressure a speaker of such importance?

The official clearly looked out of the ordinary, quite different from the rather rumpled professors who had accompanied him to the meeting. His gray hair was smartly groomed. His suit was modishly tailored. He would not have looked out of place in a Western board room. I couldn't be sure of his reaction to the question, but I thought he flushed slightly. Then, however, he smiled benevolently and began, in calm and even tones, to discuss the state of the Soviet economy.

Sitting on the seventeenth floor window sill with my back to a brilliant winter sunset, I looked around the lounge. Soviet students occupied every conceivable space. Leaving just four seats and a little leg room for speaker and guests, the students, men and women, had seized the fifty chairs and had also seated themselves on tables, window sills, and the closed keyboard of an upright piano which stood in the corner. Latecomers were squeezing the standees into shoulder-to-shoulder ranks, several students were teetering on a table in the doorway, and others leaned in a rising diagonal line over the edge of the staircase bannister, straining to hear the speaker at the other end of the long rectangular room. In all, about three hundred students were present, all of them dressed informally and some even in the blue athletic sweat suits which Russian men wear in lieu of T-shirts and jeans. It was a substantial turnout, but not an unusual one.

Like the Soviet students in the lounge I had learned of the meeting from neatly hand-lettered announcements posted near the elevators on the first floor of the dormitory and at the Juridical Faculty downtown. The poster invited "all those interested" to hear a lecturer from the Central Committee. Naturally I was interested.

I had come to MGU—*Moskovskii Gosudarstvennyi Universitet*—in September of 1965 as one of a score of Americans participating in the Soviet-American academic exchange program. My field is political science, but since there is no Department of Government at MGU I was working at the Law School, which in Moscow is called the Juridical Faculty. I was doing research on Soviet city government for my Columbia University doctoral dissertation.

Besides my research, I was interested of course in the life around me; indeed I was living part of that life. Residing in the skyscraping dormitory on Lenin Hills, I lived among

Soviet students, eating and studying with them, singing and arguing with them, going to the theater and concerts with them, and even scrubbing down the kitchen and the floors as they did.

By the time I entered the seventeenth-floor lounge to hear the Central Committee lecturer, I had been in the Soviet Union several months. In the beginning there had been problems of adjustment and orientation. For although I had toured nine Soviet cities with a group of American students during the summer of 1964, now I was on my own. My Russian language was in fine fettle when I arrived, since I had studied Russian for five years at Harvard and Columbia and had been the interpreter during the 1965 cross-country American tour of the Soviet National Basketball Team. But the crux of the problem in Moscow was not how to say something in Russian, but what to say, and how to act while living in the midst of a Communist society. And there were other questions.

What research opportunities can an American request from Soviet academic authorities, what will he get, and what should he do when he doesn't get what he wants? What should he say when he is comparing Soviet and American government in a formal report, in Russian, to Soviet professors and graduate students? And what should be his reaction when he is invited to represent the Juridical Faculty in an all–MGU musical competition by playing and singing American folk songs before an audience of a thousand Russians?

Are Soviet students cautious and even fearful about befriending an American exchange student? Or do they accept him readily and warmly? Does an American meet political agitators who challenge and berate him? On the other hand, how should he treat Russians who seem almost too eager and anxious to cultivate Americans? Need an American student worry about being tailed by the Soviet secret police? Need he worry that his Soviet friends will someday have to account for the hospitality they offered him?

And what about the Russians themselves? How do they live and what do they think about their lives? As an American I could hear Soviet opinions about the U.S.A. and discover how they treat Americans. But what do they think of China and the Chinese, about Vietnam and imperialism? How do they view Negroes and people of various other nationalities? How do they remember and understand their past and their former leader Stalin? What do they think of the Communist Party, its present policies and leaders? Was it possible for an outsider, an American at that, to get an idea of their pleasures and pains, their prides and prejudices, their regrets and fears and hopes?

Seeking answers to these questions, I took chances by entering many doors that were not closed, to meetings, lectures, and conferences where people spoke openly and frankly. One of those doors led into the seventeenth-floor lounge where the man from the Central Committee was speaking. He was one of the most important men I heard in the Soviet Union. Would he be candid or condescending? By this time I had learned that his audience would not be bored and submissive, but it was hard to believe that the students would really challenge him. Would I hear the clichés of a ritual or the lively dialogue of a freer sort of speech? I listened as the speaker spoke of Soviet agriculture. To my surprise he was beginning with astonishing candor.

"During the next Five-Year Plan we are going to spend seventy billion rubles on agriculture. Why this huge amount? Because our agriculture is in trouble. Because one Soviet farmer produces enough to feed six people, while one American farmer can feed twenty-six. I repeat, *tovarishchi* (comrades) . The American figure is twenty-six."

The speaker recited his statistics with elaborate solemnity and paused as a ripple of whispered amazement spread across the lounge. Then he continued gravely, "Climate may be one of the main causes of our trouble. But we have made mistakes, too, and we have no illusions that the overall cure will be simple or easy."

There were, however, some favorable signs. The speaker smiled. "Our farmers, I can assure you, are now determined to overcome old obstacles and move ahead." He was confident and his voice rang. "I can assure you, too, *tovarishchi,* that everywhere I went on my recent tour of the countryside, everyone had enough to eat."

The speaker still had not invited questions when suddenly he was interrupted.

"That's great. Everybody's got enough to eat. But when are we going to catch up and overtake America?" The questioner was obviously recalling Khrushchev's old boast, and his tone sounded more than a bit sarcastic to me. I noticed that several students grinned and whispered to each other, and that the speaker exchanged glances with two professors who had accompanied him. The latter looked nervous and embarrassed at the interruption. But the speaker appeared unruffled and answered calmly.

"We anticipate," he said, "that after a period of three Five-Year Plans plus four more years, we will reach the level of national wealth that the United States reached in 1965."

At this, more excited whispering in the room. Elementary arithmetic, which is the only kind I have, brought me to the conclusion that nineteen more years of economic growth would bring the U.S.S.R. to a point the U.S.A. had passed in 1965. I guessed that the students must be making the same calculation. And everyone knew that during those nineteen years the American economy would continue its growth.

"We will not catch up and overtake the United States any time soon, except in a few sectors," the speaker cut into the general noise. "And there's really no sense in predicting when we will. As far as the production of automobiles is concerned, we will probably never catch them at all."

"So much for Nikita Sergeevich Khrushchev and his scientific predictions," my seat mate on the window sill muttered ironically, but not without a certain nostalgia. Did he know I was an American, and if so did he care? Other Russian students in the room had recognized me and waved hello, apparently considering it perfectly natural for me to be there.

The speaker meanwhile concluded his opening remarks. Then he invited questions from the floor.

"What are the strategy and tactics of the international workers' movement at the present stage?" The first question. It struck me as oddly stilted until I realized that it was posed in the jargon of endless Soviet writings and speeches. Obviously I was not alone.

"Oh, no, not that one again," cried a voice of mock pain from the corner.

"That's dull," complained a student sitting under the speaker's nose in the first row.

"What is this, a seminar or something?" another demanded, apparently determined to avoid it if it was.

The clamor grew as students argued among themselves about whether the question deserved to be answered or rejected as a worn-out cliché. The professor serving as chairman of the meeting tried to restore order. Finally, the original questioner, who had been loudly defending his curiosity, decided not to pursue it and retreated into silence. So, at last, did everyone else.

Another question: "Is it true that Plisetskaya and the other artists and intellectuals sent a petition to the Central Committee opposing any rehabilitation of Stalin at the Twenty-third Party Congress?" This student was repeating a rumor that was sweeping MGU after having been spread by the Voice of America.

"No, that's not true," the speaker replied patiently. He said the Central Committee had asked the artists about it, compared their signatures with signatures on the petition, and judged the paper to be a forgery by *provocateurs.*

"If the artists didn't sign it, let them deny it publicly themselves!" A short student who was standing on a table called out the challenge.

"That's not necessary. Why should they deny it?" the lecturer snapped. Now, for the first time, he was clearly showing irritation. "Why should we have to deny every stupid false rumor that exists? As for Stalin, the Party settled his historical significance in 1956 and 1961, and Congress will not raise it again."

"Will the Congress change Volgograd back to Stalingrad?" someone asked. Was he needling the speaker or was he serious?

"Only if the local residents want to rename it," the speaker replied seriously.

"Did the local residents want to replace Stalingrad with Volgograd in the first place?" someone asked in a stage whisper. Did the speaker hear the question? If so, he chose not to bite.

"And what about publishing Stalin's books again?" someone asked.

"They're available now," the speaker answered firmly, sparking another outburst from the floor.

"No, they're not, not all of them. They're not all in the stores," objected a student.

"Well, if not, they were removed by local salespeople," said the speaker.

"But they're not all available in the libraries, either," said another student.

"Well, if not, then the local librarians removed them," replied the speaker.

By this time many students were laughing. "Who is running this country, anyway, the local people?" one boy shouted, triggering a burst of laughter and applause around him.

I was beginning to wonder who was running the meeting. The lecture had become a confrontation between speaker and audience, and the procedure of orderly questions and answers was disintegrating. My Russian was good, but I was hard pressed to keep up. No one could take in everything, but the sense of the side comments, snide remarks, and swirling eddies of conversation and argument was unmistakable. Adding to the confusion was the constant ringing of the two seventeenth-floor telephones on a reception desk just outside the door of the lounge. I doubted that much could be heard in the back of the room where, I noticed, several students were playfully poking each other, and every now and then a few paper airplanes looped and glided aloft.

For a while one of the professors who had accompanied the speaker held the students' attention with a diatribe against West German "revanchist" foreign policy. He spoke angrily, but it was obvious that the charges were long familiar to everyone in the room. And, apparently due to a problem in his throat, the obese and sweating orator approached the end of every sentence with a gasp or a gurgle, as if running out of breath and sound. He had to gulp in air every time, and the effect was increasingly comical. The result was titters and then shouts of "*kvatit* (enough)." The professor finished his remarks and sat down.

Several times during the meeting the chairman refused to entertain irreverent questions. But each time the Central Committee lecturer overruled him and took all questions that time allowed and noise didn't prevent.

"Will Khrushchev be a delegate to the coming Twenty-third Party Congress?"

I listened more attentively, for I knew the questioner to be a member of the Communist Party. I assumed that most students in the room, like the majority of Soviet youth, were members of the Komsomol (Young Communist League). But the Party itself enrolls only the elite, about twelve million of the total Soviet population, and, I was told, only about 5,500 of the more than 30,000-man student body and faculty of MGU.

"No, Khrushchev will not be there." The speaker smiled. This apparently was a question he had anticipated.

"Why not?" The questioner was polite.

"Because he is retired on a pension and no longer works." The speaker was polite, too. The audience was silent, listening.

The questioner pressed ahead. "But he is a member of the Presidium of the Supreme Soviet and was a member of the Party Central Committee."

The speaker held his ground. "Nonetheless, there is no need to consult him at the Congress."

"But Khrushchev has been a great and important figure in world history. Even if we don't like him, how can we ignore him?"

The speaker reddened. His manner, which had been almost condescending at the beginning of the exchange, was now cold. He was cutting off debate. "There is simply no need to invite pensioners. And there's no need to discuss this point further. That's that."

For a student near the door, however, that was not yet that. "But Voroshilov is a pensioner and he will be a delegate to the Congress," he shouted. Laughter erupted at this sally, snapping the tense silence. Even the speaker showed a trace of a grin as he shrugged his shoulders. "What can you do with these kids?" he said, as much to himself as anyone else.

"Are there any more questions?" the chairman asked.

There were indeed. About Indonesia—why had the Indonesian Communist Party disintegrated so suddenly? Because they listened to Chinese advice and chose a premature moment to revolt, said the speaker. About President Nasser of Egypt—was it true that he had been a Nazi during World War II and was the present Egyptian social system really socialism or was it National Socialism? The present Egyptian system was a form of socialism, replied a professor who was an expert on Middle Eastern affairs. And, no, Nasser had been too young to be a Nazi during World War II. But Nasser was twenty-one in 1941, objected a student. Well, come to think of it, said the professor, Nasser had indeed been a member of an anti-English, pro-German youth group.

About China—the speaker reported a gigantic campaign in China to teach Chinese to hate the Soviet Union. With this change in subject the atmosphere in the room changed. Students were no longer derisive; they listened attentively. Everyone seemed to be in agreement on the Chinese. Chinese students had thrown beer bottles at Soviet policemen during demonstrations in Moscow, the speaker reported. But those same Chinese students, upon returning home from advanced scientific training in Moscow, were exiled to the countryside to be purged of Soviet thinking and reeducated.

The next question was explosive. Do Party members, particularly high Party officials, get special privileges that ordinary citizens don't receive? Don't they, for instance, buy special goods in special stores? The speaker said they didn't now, although they had in the past.

"But there are special sanatoriums and camps built for high Party leaders," a student objected.

"No, there are not," the speaker insisted.

Again there was commotion as separate circles of students debated the issue. One man condemned any special privilege. But another disagreed. "Of course the top leaders have special privileges," he said. "They deserve them. After all, don't cabinet ministers in all countries have them?"

"Of course the leaders should get certain perquisites," I heard a third student say. "The trouble is not that they get them, but that they hide their privileges and deny that they have any."

The chairman tried to restore order amid the noise and confusion. Failing that, he adjourned the meeting. But students from the front rows surged forward to continue questioning the speaker, and spectators in the rear remained in the room talking among themselves. After five minutes the Central Committee lecturer looked around the room again. "Do you want to continue?" he shouted. "Or shall we go home?"

"More. More. Let's continue," came the shouts. The speaker sat down again; the students returned to their places.

The first raised hand appeared from behind a large green plant on a table near the window. The owner of the hand appeared next. He was Chinese.

"I want to reply to what the speaker said about my country." The Chinese student wore glasses and a high-buttoned blue suit. He was very small, very thin, and very nervous. Another Chinese student, also in glasses and a blue suit, and also short, thin, and tense, stood next to him. The first Chinese spoke poor but rapid Russian in a high-pitched voice.

"I want to deny the charges the speaker made about my country. It is not true that the Chinese exchange students are sent to farms to be reeducated when they return from Moscow. That is a lie. They work on their specialties in universities when they return. As for the speaker's charge that China slanders the Soviet Union, everyone knows that it is the Soviet Khrushchevist revisionist clique that slanders. . . ."

The Chinese never had a chance to finish his sentence in the turmoil which now exploded in the room.

"Throw out the Chinese," Soviet students shouted. "To hell with them."

"No, no. Let the Chinese speak," other Russians yelled.

I had begun to move toward the door when the chairman first adjourned the meeting, but found myself trapped near the piano when the speaker declared it open again. I climbed atop the piano, above the crowd, and surveyed the scene.

The Central Committee speaker and the professors had abandoned the meeting, as well as the beleaguered Chinese, and were pushing their way toward the door. The Russians, determined to evict the Chinese, were pushing toward them. The first Chinese student, sweating profusely and with eyes distended, was still shouting accusations in the center of the room, while the second Chinese stood his ground with a frightened smile.

The faces of the rougher Russians showed hate and even violence, and the Chinese raised their arms as if to ward off blows. But when the Russians reached their quarry, they merely grabbed them by the arms and hustled them out of the room.

The remaining students drifted away talking among themselves. The meeting had ended. I lowered myself from the piano, once the way was clear, and left the lounge.

Returning to my room, I mulled over the meaning of the meeting. The speaker had never really lost his Central Committee cool, even when the professors blanched before the din. Speaking on and off for over three hours, he had been poised and incredibly patient. His manner seemed to be silently telling the students that he understood their impatience and irreverence, even as they must understand the leadership's positions and problems. We are fundamentally in agreement, his whole demeanor seemed to say, even though you young, eager people think we are sometimes too cautious and too slow.

"We couldn't have had a meeting like this twenty years ago," the speaker had declared at one point, and everyone in the room understood his meaning. The very turmoil and dissent, he implied, proved how far the Soviet Union had advanced.

And yet I wondered, remembering a young Party member and the questions he put to another Party official at another crowded meeting in the university.

"I am, of course, in favor of Soviet power," said the student, rising to his feet in some embarrassment but determined to speak. "But why must we make great promises which we cannot keep? Khrushchev said we would soon overtake America and live under Communism. The leadership has been wrong so many times that now it's hard to believe anything. We say that after Khrushchev our planners have become truly scientific. But that's what they always said until the plans failed. No one ever criticized Khrushchev until he was gone. No one criticizes anyone at Party Congresses; instead one man speaks and the rest say how wonderful he is. Why is there no discussion, no real debate?"

How should I interpret the Soviet students' treatment of the Party speakers and the Party line? Did this meeting, which resembled others I attended during my stay in the Soviet Union, prove that Soviet students are discontented and disenchanted, as well as downright disrespectful toward their elders? If so, how many students and how deep was their dissatisfaction? To what Communist ends and means were they still loyal? It was hard to tell in that noisy crowded room. It was hard to know how many students had actively challenged the speaker, how many had only laughed at the jokes, and how many were ashamed of the whole spectacle. What about the students who didn't come to lectures and meetings? What did they think, and where did they fit in? Perhaps the commotion was a healthy thing, for didn't it demonstrate that speech is freer in the Soviet Union than many Americans think?

I thought about these questions as I sorted materials to take to the library the next morning. From a room somewhere near me came the muffled sound of Pete Seeger "Coming Round the Mountain" on some Soviet student's tape recorder. Finishing my work for the evening, I had no time to ponder further the significance of the meeting. I had to think instead about getting breakfast the next morning, shopping on the way downtown, meeting my Soviet academic adviser, tracing a book in the library, arranging an interview with a city official, going to the theater, and getting back to MGU in time to play my guitar at a Soviet friend's birthday party.

2

Express to the Seventeenth Floor

THE FINNAIR CARAVELLE jet touched down at Sheremetyevo Airport on a mid-September afternoon. I had arrived in Moscow for the second time. A year before I had come with a plane load of American students to spend some weeks polishing my Russian. Then four tourist guides met the hundred and thirty of us, and we were driven in four large tourist buses to four large tourist hotels.

This time I was anything but a tourist, and there was no one to meet me, it seemed, as I entered the modern glass and steel airport building. I expected to be met by a representative of the Ministry of Higher Education, which runs the exchange program on the Soviet side. But there was no representative in sight, and I began to steel myself to deal with customs agents, porters, taxi drivers, and university bureaucrats.

Presently, however, I caught sight of a young man waving at me excitedly from the other side of the customs barrier. He was my guide, it turned out, a graduate student sent to meet me by my adviser in the Juridical Faculty. He had been waiting for me in the wrong place, he explained apologetically as we gathered my luggage, which included two suitcases of winter clothing, a knapsack of boots and heavy shoes, a briefcase full of research plans, and a flight bag containing Western miracles like Scotch tape, an electric extension cord, an immersion heater made in Japan, assorted can openers, and ball-point pens, which I had been told are hard to come by in a Soviet dormitory.

Soviet customs didn't bother to open my bags and I wondered whether the omission was a courtesy or a product of the general confusion. My guide hastily picked up as many bags as he could, a kindness I particularly appreciated since I had strained my back lifting them in Stockholm. Outside the terminal a micro-bus and driver were waiting to take us to the university.

I rolled out my Russian vocabulary and attempted to chat as we drove past the fields and forest surrounding the airport. I asked my host about the Juridical Faculty, which unlike American law schools trains mostly undergraduates, as well as a few graduate students. My guide said he was writing a dissertation in the *Kafedra* or Department of Administrative Law where I, too, would be working. He told me that I had an appointment the next morning with the professor who was to be my adviser.

As we drove farther I noted, as I had a year earlier, the incredibly sharp division between city and country in Moscow. As before, the box-like prefabricated apartment houses marched almost to the edge of the forest, but even in a year's time their ranks seemed to have swelled. Moving into heavier traffic, we passed older buildings which looked shabby, belying the fact that they were only ten years old. The year before I had noted the tendency of Moscow buildings to peel and flake before their time, and now, in the bright autumn sunlight, I saw that decay was continuing. The people on the sidewalks, on the other hand, looked more colorfully and more stylishly dressed.

My guide had been silent as I examined the odd blend of

drab and vivid scenery, but his diffidence vanished when the university towers loomed into view in the distance.

"That place is so big," he said, "and it's got so many stores and services that the students say you can live for months at a time without ever going outside. And in the winter there are times when it's so cold you'd better not go outside. You'll see."

I already knew some of MGU's vital statistics, having read them in the official *University Handbook*. Moscow University, founded in 1755 by the Russian scholar Mikhail Lomonosov, is the largest and most distinguished university of the Soviet Union. It has more than thirty thousand students, of whom almost fifteen thousand are correspondence or evening-division students who hold other jobs, and about four thousand graduate students. Of MGU's thirteen divisions (called faculties in Moscow), the natural sciences faculties are located on Lenin Hills and the humanities faculties are in the old buildings near Red Square in downtown Moscow. The main complex of buildings on Lenin Hills, which was built between 1949 and 1953, also houses the dormitory for upperclassmen, while freshmen and sophomores live in an annex a few blocks away on Lomonosovskii Prospekt.

I had heard from former American exchange students about some of the stores, services, clubs, and entertainments in the Lenin Hills complex. There were two restaurants, two cafeterias, and several snack bars. There were food stores, drug stores, book stalls, shoe and watch repair shops, and a photo studio. There was a barbershop, a beauty parlor, a laundry room, a dry cleaning establishment, and a post and telegraph office, as well as newsstands and places to buy tickets to all the theaters and concert halls of Moscow. There was a gym and a swimming pool, and, in the *Dom Kul'tury* (House of Culture), an art group, a ballet studio, several theatrical groups, and other cultural clubs. And the dormitory was fully coeducational. In past years the sexes had been separated, but this year men and women lived on the same floors.

The arrangement sounded more like a Miami resort than a Communist university. But then MGU is the flagship of Soviet higher education, and the Lenin Hills complex is a showpiece and a showcase. Set back about a half mile from the Moscow River, MGU overlooks the river and the center of Moscow beyond. Between the university and the river is a great expanse of greensward with fountains and reflecting pools. Two broad avenues lead up to the bluff over the river, where there is a park, a beach for swimming, and a ski jump where competitors leap onto snow in winter and onto wet straw in spring and fall. On the opposite side of the university lies a formal garden, arranged around a statue of Lomonosov. To the left of the central complex is *sportgorodok*—sports city—with its outdoor basketball and volleyball courts (which are flooded in winter to make a huge skating rink), soccer—called *futbal* in Russian—fields, and a large field house. To the right of MGU is another formal park, which leads up to the gates of the Chinese Embassy. That park was usually closed and barred in 1965–66.

The central section of the MGU complex of buildings is a magnificent example of Stalinist architecture. It is magnificently tall, magnificently florid, and, as most of my Soviet friends agreed, magnificently ugly. A perfect monument to Stalin's megalomania and bad taste, I thought as we drove toward it; but it looked strangely impressive in the distance with the golden star above its tallest tower glistening in the sun.

I remarked to my guide that the skyscraper was as impressive as it is ugly, but he seemed embarrassed by the comment and replied that every man is entitled to his opinion. He chose to confine himself to the facts. The MGU Lenin Hills complex, he said, consists of a central tower linked to two huge symmetrical wings, which are each divided into several zones.

That the arrangement was absolutely symmetrical I confirmed to my chagrin one day later in the year when I left the central tower and headed toward what I thought was Zone V, the zone in which I lived. I walked past the familiar marble columns and took the familiar elevator to the seventeenth floor. I noticed some unfamiliar faces at the phone desk near the lounge, but the carpet covering the long corridor seemed familiar, too. I walked down the hall and turned left again toward my familiar room. I opened the outer door, which was unlocked, and looked through the open inner door into my room. There a Soviet girl in a bathrobe was combing her hair. Only then did it dawn on me that I had drifted into the opposite wing and barged into the mirror image of my room. I mumbled a horrified "excuse me" in Russian and turned to leave. But since Soviet students usually open the outer doors of dormitory rooms without knocking, the girl didn't find my entrance particularly strange; she merely asked whom I was looking for. My own room, I replied in confusion, and hurried away.

To enter MGU you must show an official pass or *propusk,* which contains the bearer's picture. Was this some kind of totalitarian control, I wondered, accustomed as I was to the open doors of an American campus? My Soviet friends, who regarded the *propusk* system as more of a nuisance than a threat, later explained its purpose. The procedure, they said, was designed to control the flow of students' friends and relatives who might be tempted to forsake crowded apartments in the city to take up illegal residence in the comfortable dormitory. I saw for myself that the system was decidedly fallible. I usually entered through the little guardhouse at the side gate together with Soviet students who flashed their *propusks* even faster than teen-agers flash their reduced-fare high school pass on the New York subway, which is to say very quickly indeed. Whether in haste or as a lark, some students ignored the attendant entirely and brushed gaily past her into the courtyard.

In fact, until I learned to relax I was about the only one who actually addressed the guardian of the gate, who more often than not was a little lady sitting on a little stool by the door. I really couldn't tell whether she was a little *old* lady, a *starushka* in Russian, or a little young woman, since she was hidden in kerchief, padded jacket, long skirt, and boots. In any case, she usually seemed pleased to be the object of some attention, and so she smiled and waved me on. In the months ahead I entered the university many times without showing my *propusk*. The attendants seemed to check more thoroughly on holidays when visitors poured into the towers. But only a few conscientious attendants, *stakhanovites* at heart and trying perhaps to overfulfill their personal Plans, checked *propusks* consistently.

There was one time when my endorsement took the place of a *propusk*. Charles H. Percy, soon to be elected senator from Illinois, was on a fact-finding tour, and I had helped to interpret for him. Deciding to visit MGU without making prior arrangments, he arrived at the main entrance only to be stopped by the attendant who demanded to see his *propusk*. Of course he had none, and the man at the door stubbornly refused to let him pass. I was summoned and was able to vouch for Percy and his party. It gave me a heady, if momentary, feeling of power.

Once past the gate my first day we had to thread our way through a casual soccer game careening around the courtyard and among students batting badminton birds back and forth without nets. I looked up once more before we went inside and noticed several stone goddesses reading their books on the central tower and two miniature Parthenons, which adorned the roof like garish decorations on a wedding cake.

Once inside I noticed only the students. They were everywhere, hurrying upstairs and down and through the halls. There were hordes of them, it seemed to me, carrying books in arms, or food in open-mesh shopping bags, or soccer balls and badminton rackets. Some men wore suits (all of dark colors, it seemed), others slacks and sports shirts, and a few of both sexes, who were off to get some exercise, had on blue athletic sweat suits. There were older men and women, too, as well as a few babies and baby carriages which were being carried up the stairs with the aid of passers-by. I noted immediately a cluster of Chinese dressed in high-buttoned blue suits, and a group of shorter Vietnamese students. Before we reached the elevators I heard several African students speaking French and English and some Latin Americans chattering in Spanish.

My guide and I approached the elevators for what I expected would be a rapid ascent to the seventeenth floor. Instead I learned a lesson which I would value the rest of my days at MGU—how to survive on the lift. My guide began by explaining the rules of the game. The four express elevators, he said, stop only at floors between nine and nineteen, while a separate bank of elevators serves the first nine floors. We were concerned only with the express.

Impressed by this rational division of labor, I heard him explaining a further refinement which the students themselves had made into an unwritten law.

"When the first express car arrives," he said, "the students designate it as a super express. They call out *vyshe* (higher), which means that this car will stop only at the fifteenth floor or higher. Anyone who wants to get off between nine and fourteen waits for the second car and calls out *nizhe* (lower)."

As I tried to assimilate this information, I waited with a rapidly growing crowd of students for the first or *vyshe* car to present itself. After five minutes a light flashed over one door, signaling its arrival. Immediately the unwritten rules broke down. Everyone around me began to shout both *vyshe* and *nizhe* and to push toward the door. I thought for a moment that I had fallen into an angry mob. Were these the hard-pressed violent Russians I had read about in the West, the people who must struggle desperately to get a share of goods and services in short supply?

The students around me were struggling all right, but many of them were laughing too. "One passenger over the Plan! Two over the Plan! Three over! Plan overfulfilled! BONUS!" shouted somebody and they laughed even louder.

The merriment grew when the doors opened to reveal another mob who had been jammed together in the car on the way down. Though they were leaving, the beleaguered occupants of the car burst into the hall shouting *vyshe* and *nizhe,* too, apparently as a ploy to confuse the passengers waiting for the lift. In the midst of the good-natured bedlam, I somehow managed to push my way into the *vyshe* elevator.

Inside the lift a tall husky boy had pushed all the buttons from fifteen to nineteen to accommodate the *vyshe* riders. But before the doors could close a slender girl reached out to press ten.

"Oh, no, *devushka* (girl), no, you don't," the tall student said, pushing a smaller knob which released the tenth floor button.

"Is that so, is that really so?" snapped the girl, pressing ten again.

"Come on, *devushka,* this is *vyshe.* You take the next car, which'll be *nizhe.*" The master of the buttons had spoken as if to a first-grader and everyone in the elevator grinned. Everyone, that is, except the other girls in the car, who looked collectively insulted, and one harried passenger who was holding an open mesh bag of eggs high over his head to protect them from the crush.

The girl stood her ground, pressing ten again each time the boy flipped it off. Before the *vyshe* riders could stop laughing and get angry, the next car arrived and the girl retreated. But by this time so many people had surged into our car that the door wouldn't close. The tall boy pushed it, a shorter boy kicked it, a few students reluctantly got out, and finally we began our non-stop ascent to the fifteenth floor.

On the tenth floor the elevator stopped unexpectedly. The doors opened. "Oh, no," our passengers moaned. Two students stood in the doorway holding bottles of *kefir,* a dairy drink something like yogurt which they had bought at the *bufet* or canteen on the tenth floor.

"Kefirniki," someone in our car identified the strangers sorrowfully. The *kefirniki* had ruined our trip by innocently calling for the elevator. Now they expected to take it to the thirteenth floor—a stop that definitely was not included in our plans.

"But this is *vyshe,* for God's sake," the tall boy cried out. "Take the *nizhe* lift on the other side."

Sure enough, the *nizhe* lift was waiting across the hall and the *kefirniki* turned toward it. As our doors closed again, I caught sight of the slender girl we had rebuffed on the ground floor. Having reached her destination, she was standing in the hall laughing last and best at us.

We reached the seventeenth floor without further incident. Heading down the long corridor toward my room, we passed one of the three kitchens located on every floor. By this time it was after six o'clock and the kitchen was filled with so many cooks that I wondered whether they would spoil the borsch. All four burners on both gas stoves were occupied with pots and pans, and young men and women stood watching them, gossiping or washing dishes in the three sinks. In one corner of the room a sweat-suited male was ironing what appeared to be a sports jacket on the community ironing board.

"You can buy food in the food stores downstairs and cook your own meals here," said my guide, "or you can eat downstairs in one of the *stolovaias* (dining rooms). Many of the students cook for themselves because it's faster and cheaper."

Leaving the kitchen, we turned left at a large luxuriant green plant, which sits in front of a corridor window, and approached my *blok*. A *blok* consists of two bedrooms, a sink and shower room, and a toilet, all opening off a little vestibule. I was to have one bedroom to myself and a *sosed*—neighbor—would live in the other room of the *blok*.

As we stepped into the vestibule and approached my room, I heard the unmistakable music of "I've Been Working on the Railroad," as well as a loud thumping noise, coming from the other room. Just before I opened my door, something crashed into the other door and it was flung open.

A big Russian holding a soccer ball in his hand stood in the doorway. "*Zdravstvuite* (hello). How do you do? I'm your *sosed*," he said. And then, because Dinah was blowing her horn so loud we couldn't hear each other, he went back into his room to turn down his tape recorder.

3

Your Room and How to Clean It

As I looked around my room and out its window, I saw the embassy of the People's Republic of China, a graceful modern building of glass and concrete at the end of the park across the street from MGU's side gate.

I knew the Chinese charge that the Russians are turning soft and bourgeois; looking around, I decided that my room, at least, would be soft enough for a representative of the bourgeoisie. About nine feet by sixteen feet, the room contained a desk; a small dining table with an oilcloth cover; a large bookcase with sliding glass panels to protect each shelf; a closet with extra shelves; and a day bed complete with blankets, bedspread, and sheets, which were exchanged for clean ones every ten days. In addition, I was given a table lamp, a small Oriental rug, short white window curtains, and a *chainik* or tea kettle.

Since my room had far more furnishings than I ever received in a Harvard dormitory, I must have looked impressed.

"All this is standard equipment," my guide said proudly. The room next to mine was identical and every *blok* had its own bathroom.

My athletic *sosed* later admitted a bit sheepishly that he had been working out in my empty room, using it as his "private gymnasium" since returning to the university in early September. "I lost a gym but gained a capitalist," he said with a cheerful grin.

My room might do for one capitalist, but American exchange students who brought their wives to Moscow were given a whole *blok* to themselves. Soviet couples, on the other hand, usually lived in one room of a *blok,* even when there was a baby, and because of a shortage of space other students had to double up. A crowded room like that must have been uncomfortable, but I never heard a Soviet student complain. The MGU dormitory was the best in the country, they said, and anyway they didn't have a room of their own at home, either. Furthermore, when, as sometimes happened—I knew of several cases—the roommates were male and female and unmarried, the (strictly unofficial) arrangement must have been quite cozy.

Soviet students pay nothing or next to nothing for their rooms, and tuition is free. In addition, most get stipends of thirty-five to forty rubles (one ruble is worth $1.11 at official exchange rate) with which they pay for food, books, and other expenses. Students getting all "excellents" get a twenty-five percent bonus, and graduate students get much more depending on stage of training.

I was somewhat chastened to hear this, since I was going to receive a stipend of a hundred and fifty rubles a month from the Soviet government. My stipend was comparable to what Soviet exchange students in America receive from the American government, but it sounded extravagant in the Soviet setting. As it turned out, I used all the hundred and fifty as well as my own money, what with buying books and mailing them home, going to the theater regularly, and appeasing my palate now and then in expensive restaurants. Then I began to wonder how a Soviet student could ever get by on his stipend. Some people managed to do so, my Soviet friends assured me, only by watching every kopeck. Most students, I was told, supplement their stipends with help from home or by working summers and during the school year.

The one thing MGU students don't seem to do to add to their income is just what so many American students do. They don't want to work around the dormitory. My Soviet friends were amazed to learn that many Columbia undergraduates wait on tables, and some Harvard men get down on their hands and knees to clean rooms for pay.

"If we have to scrub floors for pay," a Russian once told me, "most of us would probably rather do it in the subway at night than here in the dormitory where our friends can see us. We'd really prefer to do a truly productive job, even if it's harder work."

Why do many Soviet students consider menial work to be so demeaning? Probably because the Communist Party for so long made heroes of blue-collar workers and denigrated service personnel in word and pay. At any rate, the students at MGU were glad to leave the big monthly *natirka* or floor polishing to two Amazon-like young women, not students of course, who worked with buckets of water and heavy electric floor polishers. Residents were expected to prepare for the *natirka* by piling all their furniture except the bookcase on top of their beds by 9:00 A.M. of the big day. And if anyone overslept he was liable to be awakened by the *kommandantsha* of the floor, a gray-haired grandmotherly woman who beat on the door yelling, "Wake up, *tovarishchi,* and get ready for the *natirka.*" The first time I heard that cry I was distressed, since I took the whole procedure quite seriously. I tore out of bed, threw on my clothes, piled my chairs and tables upside down on my bed, and got ready to welcome the floor polishers—who didn't come until two hours later. After the same thing happened two months in a row, I got the hang of the procedure and relaxed. The only time I minded turning the place upside down was when the *natirka* took place on December 25, obviously not a holiday in the Soviet Union.

But the *natirka* came but once a month and the rest of the time students were expected to keep their rooms clean. That was their responsibility to the collective as well as to themselves, and it was my obligation too. One of the women who supervised our floor told me about that the very first week.

She greeted me in a dignified way, looked me over slowly and carefully, and then recited the responsibilities of a resident. "You will clean your own room, and you and your *sosed* will keep the shower and toilet clean. Once a month you will have *dezhurstvo* (hall duty), along with two other students. That day you will have to get up early to mop the kitchen and dust the corridor, and then you will answer the phones in the hall for a five-hour shift."

Was the sober supervisor aware that if I did all these things carefully and conscientiously I would be practically unique on the floor? That's what I wondered later when I saw how erratically many students wielded the broom. But the first time I took in everything she said as if it were the Sermon on the Mount.

"I know you Americans are a clean and tidy people, as are most of our young people," said the good woman generously. "But just to make sure, we have a student *sankomissiia* (sanitary commission) which inspects the rooms and grades them for cleanliness and good order. I'm sure you won't have any trouble with them."

I too was sure I could keep my quarters clean, but I wondered nonetheless how a *sankomissiia* of Russian and, for all I knew, Chinese and Vietnamese students would treat an American resident in their midst.

"Oh, don't worry about that," said my *sosed* when I asked his opinion. "Since our *blok* consists of one American and one Russian room, we are subject only to international law and inspections by the United Nations. And if the *komissiia* gets tough, you can always claim extraterritoriality."

My neighbor was partially right. When the *sankomissiia* came, it came to chat as much as to inspect. A lanky law student who was *starosta* or elder of the floor poked his head under the bed looking for dust. I was startled to hear his muffled voice asking how much a 1966 Chevrolet costs in America. A female member of the *komissiia* brushed her hand across my lampshade trying to detect dust, then stood on a chair to look on top of the bookcase. "What do American girls think of mini-skirts?" she asked. A third *komissiia* member looked under my rug and muttered something about rugs probably being cheaper in America. The inspection was over. The *sankomissiia* stood at the door apparently reluctant to go. "At what age do most Americans get married?" the *studentka*—female student—asked as they departed.

I got high grades when the results of the inspections were posted in the hall near the lounge. Was my room really that exemplary, or were the inspectors pleased to gossip with an American? In any case, when the inspections suddenly ceased, after a famous coup d'état, I actually missed their bonhomie.

The coup took place because the *sankomissiia* had been tougher on Soviet students than it had been on me, and it had made enemies. Its enemies combined at a meeting of the floor committee to oust the *komissiia* leadership and put in men and women who were less exigent. Perhaps they were inclined to let dust accumulate on their own lampshades. At any rate, they would not condemn others for doing the same.

But then came the counterattack, in which the old leadership, aided by the Faculty administration, regained control. A meeting was called in the lounge and a woman professor of criminal law came from the Faculty to address the assembled sinners and a few kibitzers, too.

"I have looked around your rooms," said the professor,

"and I don't know how some of you can live in such a mess. I think the well-known coup was disgraceful."

"If you don't punish us, we won't do anything," retorted a Georgian student, evoking wild laughter from students who are taught that collective public opinion and not compulsion should move men in a Communist society.

"Some of these students get up at eleven o'clock in the morning," said one of the elderly cleaning ladies who had to clean up after the students. "I've seen them and I don't mind telling you I think it's immoral."

"They get up late because they play cards in the lounge at one o'clock in the morning," put in another woman who was the night *kommandantsha.* "And when we try to close the lounge and tell them to go to bed, you should hear the things they say to us. They say if playing cards are sold, why can't they play with them? They ask us what article of the Soviet Criminal Code prohibits playing cards in the MGU lounge at one o'clock in the morning."

"We were just playing *durochka* (little idiot)," interrupted one of the students, convulsing the rest of the students with laughter. "We really wanted to play chess. [More laughter.] But we could only find the cards. Why should they lock up the lounge so early? Students need a place to relax after they finish studying."

"Studying? Bah!" grumbled the night *kommandanstsha.*

Eventually the meeting got around again to its original theme, the *san-inspektsii.* The woman professor seemed more sad than angry, but she warned that future offenders would be punished by the Faculty. The head of the student committee exhorted his comrades to repent, and in the end the coup was repudiated and the students agreed to live more cleanly ever after.

But as a witness to the affair, I doubted that the original coup was wholly directed against inspections, since the formal charges leveled against the old leadership had had nothing to do with cleanliness at all. Instead, like Stalin, the old guard was accused, in suitable jargon, of "violating norms of socialist democracy" and "manifesting excessive and dangerous centralism." Like Khrushchev, the conscientious inspectors had been guilty of "subjectivism" and "harebrained scheming." The word was passed solemnly that the sacred socialist principle of "democratic centralism" demanded a democratic overthrow of the central leadership, something, it was admitted, that this sacred principle has not demanded too often in the history of the Communist Party.

The plotters intoned these clichés with such relish and good humor that I began to suspect that they had pulled the coup more for the fun of playing with old political pieties than to rid themselves of the inspections. Almost all the residents of my floor were students of government and law at the Juridical Faculty, which meant that they had to use political jargon more than chemists or math majors do. Since the chemists and mathematicians seemed to be enduring rigorous inspection on their floor, I concluded that the jurists couldn't resist the temptation to put their subject matter to practical use.

But I've been running ahead of myself. Practical advice was what I needed as I stood chatting in my room on my first day in Moscow. I could smell the most tempting aromas coming from the kitchen down the hall, and I hadn't eaten since Finland.

"To get to the *studencheskaia stolovaia,*" said my guide, who had another engagement for dinner, "just take the elevator down to the main floor and then walk down to the basement of Zone V. Or, if you prefer, there's another *stolovaia* just like it in Zone B."

I thanked my guide for his help. "*Do svidaniia* (goodbye)," he said, and left me alone.

4

Board and How to Get It

ALONE in Moscow for the first time, I felt both exhilaration and doubt. I was pleased with my quarters and eager to plunge into university life. But I wondered what kind of reception I would find as an American.

I left my room and headed for the *stolovaia* the first evening thinking anxious thoughts, but the elevator brought me down to earth immediately. For the MGU elevators are not only great raisers and lowerers of men, but great levelers as well. If I expected to be treated as anything but a simple, ordinary passenger, I was romanticizing my situation. The elevator, I learned again, has a life of its own, demands discipline from its riders, and accepts neither nationality nor sentimentality as relevant.

When it arrived on the seventeenth floor at about 7 P.M., the lift was nearly full. I managed to get in without any difficulty, but I braced myself for what other floors would bring. On the sixteenth floor the car stopped and the doors opened. A small throng was waiting.

"We're full up," announced a student in our car who was standing near the control buttons. "But there's another lift coming in just a minute on the other side. *Eto pravda* (that's the truth)."

The students on the landing looked skeptical, as if they had heard that line too many times before. Lowering their heads, four men charged. One managed to wedge himself in, three fell back, and finally we set off again.

The fifteenth floor. The scene was the same; only the students hoping to get in our car were different. They must have been more gentle or more gullible souls, for they accepted our leader's assurance that another lift was coming, stepped back politely, and permitted us to continue our trip. Our crowd was exultant.

"Give them the same treatment on the fourteenth," someone shouted, "only with more spirit."

This our captain did, gaining confidence and authority at each stop, and easily convincing the waiting students that another lift was coming, which by now it probably was. We congratulated ourselves each time, plummeted the last nine stories triumphantly without a stop, and arrived a small happy community of survivors of a common ordeal.

I shared the exhilaration even though, as a neophyte, I was a bit shaken. But in the months that followed I learned to look forward to traveling the lift. It had its rush hours, during the morning and evening, and its quiet hours free of crises and tension. In the afternoon even an American could take command. I remember the heady feeling I had the first time I intimidated a few *nizhe* travelers by gruffly shouting, "*Vyshe, tovarishchi, vyshe.* Don't you know the first car is always *vyshe?*" To my surprise they yielded the car to me and I had a nonstop ride to the seventeenth floor.

Of course I lost a few battles too, including several defeats at the hands of an aggressive eight-year-old boy from Soviet Control Asia who always seemed to run up just in time to yell *nizhe* before anyone could rightfully claim the first car as *vyshe.* The son of a student couple living in the dorm, the boy could defy the unwritten laws because no grownup could resist either his grin or the sight of him on a tricycle scooting along the fifth-floor corridor. The only riders who could defeat him were older kids who sometimes sneaked into the university to ride the elevators for fun. These worthies, who looked like players from "Our Gang" comedies in their oversized suits and peaked caps, traveled transfixed before the panel of buttons, riding up and down in wonder. They made things uncomfortable for serious commuters, who, nonetheless, usually trated them with affection. Like so many Russians, the elevator riders could not be stern with children. And several Russians told me that the urchins in the elevator were like the *prostoi russkii narod,* the simple people of Russia who greet the achievements of twentieth-century science and technology as much with wonder as with pride and satisfaction.

My first glimpse of the *studencheskaia stolovaia* filled me with wonder but with little else. Four lines of students waited to approach four cashiers' booths outside the *stolovaia,* and there were two more lines inside the cafeteria. The students on line, like those in the elevator, were preoccupied with their own affairs. It was up to me to figure out the system if I were to get anything to eat. I joined a line and waited.

As our queue inched forward, I noticed a menu posted next to the cashier's window. When students reached the window, they read the menu, called out their selections, and then waited as the cashier, a big blond woman dressed in a white smock, punched them out on a cash register. The register printed the chits, but did not add up the total, a computation that was the job of the cashier's abacus. (The abacus, by the way, is still used in most restaurants and stores in Moscow.) Finally the cashier accepted the money, made change rather reluctantly, and growled, *"Shto vy khotite molodoi chelovek?* (What do you want young man?) " to the next in line.

By the time I had taken in the complex procedure, I found myself standing by the window; and suddenly I heard the gruff voice telling me to order. I looked at the menu, which was a smeared carbon copy, and those words not smudged, I didn't understand. The cashier growled again and so, though I didn't see them on the menu, I took a stab at borsch and *salat*. To my relief, she punched them out without comment. Then I mispronounced a dish, and she ordered me to repeat it and hurry up about it, too. I looked back at those behind me and up into the harried unsympathetic face in the booth. In wordless desperation, I pointed to a smudge on the menu.

"That's *podzharka,* a meat dish," put in a young man behind me helpfully.

I repeated the word and the cashier punched it out.

"What else do you want?" she snorted.

"Nichevo," I said. (Nothing.)

"What about soup? Don't you want some *kefir,* some bread?" The plump cashier was apparently melting a bit at the prospect of thin *tovarishch's* going hungry.

"Nu ladno," I said. "All right. Let's have some soup, *kefir* and bread too."

The cashier turned to the abacus, flicked its buttons back and forth with astonishing speed and announced that I owed her seventy kopecks for the whole meal. I paid her.

Inside the *stolovaia* I discovered two lines of students who were waiting to reach the food counter. I was tired by this time, I was beginning to be rather discouraged about lines and delays. I thought some of the Soviet students seemed as disheartened as I as they waited silently. But others were chatting gaily, while still more huddled together in little groups examining and trading chits like busy brokers on the stock exchange floor. They were conspiring to beat the system by speeding it up. Their method, like the unwritten code of the elevators, was founded on the specialization of labor; but it depended as well on another crucial unwritten rule, which decrees that anyone may join any friend in line at any time. While one student stood in a cashier's-booth line to buy chits for his group, his friends waited in the food-counter line, saving a place for him. Their timing was good, for the man with chits arrived just as his friends reached the food counter. There the chits were distributed so that each student could specialize. One gathered soups for all, another got salad, a third rounded up drinks, and a fourth collected bread and utensils. (Knives, however, were seldom available in the *stolovaia,* perhaps because they were very available in some students' rooms.)

I had to collect my food myself at the counter, trading a chit for every dish. Luckily the girl recognized *podzharka* by its price, for I had long since forgotten its name and dreaded another confrontation with an impatient counter woman.

There were no empty tables, so I decided to sit down next to two girls. I asked and received their permission, and then I ate in silence as they gossiped about friends they didn't seem to like and enemies they did. I was eager to talk, to begin meeting people; and, besides, I needed some elementary information.

"Excuse me," I began, "but can you tell me the name of the dish you are eating? I'm new here, you see."

The *studentki* looked at me rather coolly and then at each other. One of them answered politely.

"Kotlety," she said. (Cutlets.)

The girls resumed their conversation and paid no more attention to me. I was surprised because I knew from my earlier trip that Soviet young people can be very informal. I remembered how, a year ago, I had struck up innumerable conversations by asking a simple question and casually mentioning my nationality. This time I was resolved not to wave the flag, yet I was very tempted. I decided on a subtle route.

"Excuse me again," I said, "but are there always such long lines here? You see, I'm a foreigner and I just arrived today."

I assumed that this modest sally would at least prompt them to ask how foreign I was and where I had come from.

"Well, the lines are pretty bad at rush hour," one of the girls said, "but it isn't bad at all after eight o'clock."

The *studentki* smiled and continued their conversation again without me, and I wondered why. Was their reticence political? Were they reluctant to converse with a foreigner in a public place? Or did they think me rude? Did they think I was trying to pick them up or put them on? Or were they just tired after a day's work and concerned with their own affairs? I didn't know. But I resolved to eat in the future in a *stolovaia* on the second floor where the atmosphere was supposed to be less hectic and more convivial.

There were two *stolovaias* on the second floor of the central tower of MGU: the *dieticheskaia*—dietetic—*stolovaia* offered a fare of mild and moderately greaseless food, and the *professorskaia stolovaia* offered some reserved seats for professors during luncheon. The food was better (and more expensive, too) in both places than in the basements of Zones B and V, and the tables were set and served by pleasant waitresses. The only trouble was that a customer often had to stand in line to buy chits and then in another queue waiting for a seat. Nonetheless I was full of hope the first time, for I was the tenth man from the cashier's window.

The line to the window, however, neither shortened in front of me nor did it lengthen behind me. Instead it *thickened* between me and the window. One at a time students walked up to their friends in front of me, shook hands, and joined them. Soon friends were joining friends of friends as if the line were a New Year's Eve party, and soon the knots of people were actually pushing me farther away from the cashier. In desperation I complained to three girls in front of me that at this rate a foreigner without friends might starve to death in the hallway. They giggled and blushed and led me to the front of the line. For a moment I feared they were going to make a protest to the management on my behalf or a request to the people heading the line to make room for me. But before I could explain that I wanted no special treatment, I saw they were simply shaking hands with a friend of theirs who had joined a friend of his who was first in line. I shook hands all around too. Then we all bought chits, stood briefly waiting for a seat, and entered the restaurant.

When we had seated ourselves at a table, one of the students asked me where I was from. From the U.S.A., I answered, not knowing what reaction to expect.

"*Slushaite mal'chiki, devchonki* (listen, boys and girls)," he called to his friends at the table, "this guy's a *'Shtatnik.'* "

"Where in the States?" another student asked.

"New York City," I replied.

"New York City itself, eh? That's really something, to be eating dinner in the *stolovaia* with a New Yorker."

The girls giggled again and everyone smiled; but before I could ask where they were from, the boys got sidetracked into an argument about chemistry, which I took to be their specialty. Meanwhile I noticed that everyone in the room was eating rapidly, as if pressured by the hungry presence of people who were waiting in the doorway for seats. By the time the students had agreed on the right chemical formula, the waitress was bringing dessert. One student asked how I had come and what I was studying, and were there any Russians studying in the U.S.? Then it was time to make way for the next shift of diners. As we left, the students wished me luck and said they hoped we'd meet again. "Preferably when one of us is near the front of the line," I said, and they laughed. Then they hurried away.

Throughout the year at MGU I had many glancing encounters of this kind in the *stolovaias*. Though always polite, strangers were rarely enthusiastic or excited in the restaurant. Even some students who were warm and friendly in their rooms seemed reluctant to socialize with an American in the *stolovaia*. In the beginning of the year I was puzzled and disappointed. But I decided not to leap to any conclusions. I concentrated on getting fed. The only trouble was that I still lacked a man's best friend, someone up front in a line. The problem was particularly acute at the *dieticheskaia* and *professorskaia* because droves of foreign students with generous stipends patronized those places whose prices (around a ruble for dinner) many Soviet students didn't want to pay. Soviet students couldn't help but notice that among the restaurants' steadiest customers were well-heeled students from poor and underdeveloped Asia, Africa, and Latin America. I couldn't help but notice that one Arab in front of me in line meant there would soon be ten more.

How good was the food in university *stolovaias?* Compared with American institutional fare—the only fair comparison—the portions of meat were smaller and often tougher, and the portions of potatoes and cooked cabbage were bigger. Fresh vegetables—except for carrots—were rare in winter and so was fresh fruit—although apples and oranges were available in the stores. There was plenty of fresh bread, rich soups, hot tea, *kefir* and *smetana* (sour cream), and a meat and potato salad that was quite good. Excellent wines from Soviet Georgia were available and so was Soviet beer, served warm, but a mob at the counter usually meant Czech or Polish beer was on sale. The prices were reasonable, especially in the *studencheskie stolovaias,* and the timetable of service was helpful too: you could eat a meal of many courses at almost any time between 7:30 A.M. and 9:30 P.M., assuming you wanted to eat a meal of many courses that early in the morning. And if you lunched before 11:30 or after 3:00, and ate supper before 5:30 or after 8:00, you might well miss the lines.

Students could and did fall back on the food stores and community kitchens in the dorms. Milk and bread were cheap (fifteen kopecks a bottle, and as low as fourteen kopecks a loaf), but fresh apples and oranges were expensive (one ruble fifty kopecks for a kilo). All kinds of cheeses, meats, canned vegetables, juices, and fish, and, occasionally, fresh fish were available, too. Most of the men I saw in the kitchens seemed to specialize in fried potatoes, but they knew how to cook more interesting concoctions when they had more time. All the *studentki* I knew were excellent cooks.

I was able to supplement my diet with food from the American Embassy Commissary and with treasures from Moscow's special "dollar" food store, which sells the best Soviet produce as well as Western goods for dollars and other freely convertible foreign currencies. The dollar store had things like bananas and lettuce and tomatoes when Soviet stores didn't, and most goods cost half as much in dollars as in rubles. A bottle of Scotch costs only two dollars. Lacking dollars, Soviet students couldn't use the dollar stores, and I wondered whether they resented the double standard. Those who mentioned the matter to me seemed to think the system was justified. "The country needs foreign exchange," said one student, "and this is one way to get it."

For Soviet students food packages from home were welcome, especially when the family owned a private garden plot and cow. A friend of mine whose family lived sixty miles from Moscow went home periodically. He left MGU in the evening and returned just before dawn, so as not to miss classes, and brought back fresh milk, curds, and his mother's fruit preserves, which he insisted I share with him. The only trouble was that since the Soviet Union lacks twist-top jars, the precious produce spilled in his knapsack en route. We solved that problem with American twist-top jars from the Embassy Commissary and the Soviet dollar store. He carried the curds in an empty peanut butter jar, the preserves in a jar formerly containing Tang, and milk in a bottle formerly dedicated to Ballantine's Scotch. His mother appreciated the jars, too, for she appropriated several for next year's preserves. Thus we breakfasted royally, at least once a month. In the spring when the thaw made roads virtually impassable, my friend's father came to the dorm with his high boots so that he could continue his journeys home and back through the mud.

MGU students were often downtown at meal time, and the choice of eating places was limited. Food was cheap at the downtown campus cafeterias, but these *stolovaias* were small and crowded during the brief break between classes. The *stolovaia* at Lenin Library was particularly depressing, since the crush of customers apparently left the staff little time to keep the place clean. There were a number of small but pleasant cafés and snack bars downtown, but not enough. And in the larger and more elegant restaurants, prices were too high and service too slow for busy students.

With my generous stipend I was able to splurge two or three rubles on dinner in one of the excellent restaurants which serve the specialities of Soviet republics such as Armenia, Georgia, and Azerbaijan, and Soviet allies such as Czechoslovakia and Hungary. (The Chinese dishes at the Hotel Peking were one casualty of the Sino-Soviet dispute: they were quite unappetizing, apparently because the Chinese chef had been called home.) But even the best places presented problems. I tried the restaurant at *Dom Druzhby,* the House of Friendship with Peoples of Foreign Nations. But at first I found neither friendship nor a restaurant. I dropped in the day after a Canadian friend had eaten there and had raved about the food and service. But a gruff doorman who was built like a bouncer told me the restaurant was closed for repairs and almost threw me out forcibly. Was this a case of here today—under repair tomorrow? Apparently so, for when I returned a month later I found a pleasant newly redone restaurant complete with long wooden tables, red brick walls, efficient cheerful waitresses, and a clientele of nattily dressed Russians who looked as much like swingers as anyone I ever saw in Moscow. Unfortunately there were no seats to be had.

There were plenty of seats and good food, too, at the second-floor restaurant of the elegant National Hotel—if you could just get to them. The doorman at the side door always barred the way, saying the restaurant was closed. And the man at the front entrance usually refused, on the same ground, to accept my coat in the cloakroom. If I named the bar or barbershop as my destination, however, my coat was taken, the coast was clear, and I almost always found the restaurant open and eager for business. Why then the great charade? When I asked about the restaurant in English, even the man at the side door let me in. I concluded they were saving seats for foreign tourists.

Nobody was saving seats for foreign tourists at places like the simple *stolovaia* which I reached through a muddy courtyard off Prospekt Kalinina. This cafeteria, which served ordinary Russians, was hot and crowded, especially the day a mob of school kids turned the place upside down. They piled all their coats up to the ceiling in the hallway, and then roared into the dining room snarling the queues for chits and food, and grabbing most of the seats. Gulping my soup in a neutral corner, I expected at any moment to see someone lose his temper. One of the girls behind the counter did blow up and berate the customers, but the big red-faced cook in a dirty apron just chopped cabbage and tossed it into the soup a little faster, and a tiny kerchiefed creature in the kitchen only strained and stretched a little harder to stir the soup in a black kettle that was far larger than she. Most of the older customers continued eating as best they could under the circumstances.

How could Russians remain so patient and good-humored in the face of crowds and poor service? "Well, you might say we have no choice," said one student bitterly.

"We're used to shortages and lines," said another, who was a Party member. "Things were much worse before the Revolution, and during the war some people had nothing to eat.

We put up with a lot of poor service while we built the heavy industry we need. Now the Party is promising many more consumers' goods and is trying to improve services. Nobody I know is against that."

"Standing in line is good for you," said a third student with a wink. "You Americans are too soft. Things come too easily for you. Don't you know that food tastes better when you have to work for it?"

5

The Scholarly Life

THE Juridical Faculty of MGU is a few blocks from the Kremlin on Herzen Street, a thirty-minute ride by bus from Lenin Hills. But riding the bus demands even more discipline and dedication than riding the MGU elevator.

The buses don't look very different from American buses—just a little shorter and squatter—but the rules of the game require some study. Passengers board through the rear door, since they have little concourse with the driver, who sits in a closed-off cab and interrupts his driving only to sell *abonementnye knizhki*—commutation tickets—and to exhort passengers, over the loudspeaker system, to pay the five-kopeck fare. Since there is no conductor, riders take care of themselves, dropping fares in a cylindrical coin box and tearing tickets from a roll. The procedure runs on the honor system except when an inspector passes through. Passengers sitting near the coin box are supposed to act as volunteer inspectors, but as far as I could see, relatively few riders—usually women—took on that responsibility.

If the rider has a prepaid book of tickets or exact change, paying the fare is no problem. Otherwise, he must begin doing business with his fellow passengers. "*Ne brosaite piat' kopeek!* (Don't throw your five kopecks!)" shouts the rider who has only a ten-kopeck piece and needs five kopecks change from the next passenger. The unfortunate who has only a twenty-five-kopeck coin becomes, in effect, a temporary employee of the state. He has to negotiate his change from the next four passengers. What happens when the fare is four kopecks—as it is on an electric *trolleibus*—and all you have is a twenty-five-kopeck piece? How do you get twenty-one kopecks change? In theory, you deposit the twenty-five kopecks in the coin box, collect four-kopeck fares from each of the next six passengers—after telling each of them not to *brosat'* his fare—drop three of those kopecks in the coin box, and keep twenty-one kopecks as change. That's what you should do. But the first time I was confronted with this problem I panicked. I was only going a short way so I had to watch for my stop, and two *babushkas*—grandmothers—were eyeing me suspiciously to see if I was intending to cheat the U.S.S.R. I couldn't even figure out what I had to do, let alone do it. I simply dropped in my twenty-five-kopeck piece, took my ticket, looked frantically for my stop, and got off leaving a twenty-one-kopeck windfall for the Moscow Transit System and a couple of *babushkas* wondering what kind of fool I was.

The problems of riding the bus were multiplied during rush hour when the crush was sometimes so fierce that a rider's feet barely touched the floor. Then passengers passed tickets and change from hand to hand like buckets on a fire brigade. And long before his stop, a rider who wanted to get off had to begin asking everyone between him and the door whether he or she was also intending to debark. The trick to rush-hour bus riding, I learned from Soviet students, is to get on at the first stop, take a window seat, and sit staring out the window. That way you hardly notice the mob; and even if you are tempted to yield your seat to an elderly lady, it is physically impossible to move, which is fine until you have to get off.

Usually I took the metro or subway, which, as most Westerners know, is the pride of Moscow. The metro fare is five kopecks, which may be painlessly placed in an automatic turnstile. And though the metro also is crowded at rush hours —even more crowded than in New York, perhaps because Moscow has fewer private cars—at least the ride doesn't last so long as the bus.

The Juridical Faculty is housed in a building that looks as if it dates to the time the university was founded. Like the other humanities faculties, it is waiting for a new building to be completed on Lenin Hills. "The natural sciences moved out first," said a professor of law, "because the authorities think the sciences are more important. The Rector isn't even sure yet whether geography is a science."

The Juridical Faculty is more than a law school, for it is concerned with "State and Law." Most of its *kafedras* are traditional legal ones (Criminal Law, Civil Law, Labor Law, Land Law), but at least two deal with problems of political science (State Law and Soviet Construction, and Administrative Law). The Faculty's graduate students study for a *kandidat* degree, which is somewhere between an American master's and doctorate. The Soviet doctorate is a senior, distinguished degree which scholars get in their thirties, forties, or later. But most students are undergraduates who take a five-year course to prepare for careers as lawyers, judges, prosecutors, law enforcement officials, and cadres in economic enterprises and state bureaucracies. The undergraduate curriculum is dominated by required legal subjects. But there are a few electives, as well as required courses in Political Economy, History of the Communist Party, Fundamentals of Scientific Communism and Marxist-Leninist Philosophy, which are also taken by students of other faculties.

Admission to all MGU faculties is by competitive examinations, and the competition is stiff. In 1966 there were 13,000 applicants for 1,900 places in the natural sciences faculties, and there were six applicants for every place in the humanities. Applicants come to Moscow in the summer from all over the Soviet Union to submit to the battery of entrance exams, which includes tests in the student's specialty, a foreign language (English, German, or French), and Russian language and literature. MGU holds its entrance exams a month before other Soviet universities and institutes to give those who fail a chance to apply elsewhere. Students who just miss getting into MGU often are accepted by other institutions without having to take additional exams.

Approximately half the freshmen admitted by MGU come from the Moscow area and the rest, from every part of the country. Army veterans are admitted on the basis of a noncompetitive exam, or even without an exam, if they have credits toward a university degree. Honors high school graduates take only an exam in their special field and are admitted automatically if they pass with "excellents." In Khrushchev's time, applicants who had worked at least two years after high school had priority; eighty percent of university places were saved for them, and only they could be admitted to study law, philology, journalism, and political economy. As late as 1964, only twenty percent of MGU freshmen came directly from high school. But then the system was changed because, as the Minister of Higher Education said in March, 1965, "We had been compelled to reject [qualified] high school graduates and admit poorly prepared production workers." In 1965, some eighty percent of freshmen came straight from school.

The Mechanical-Mathematics Faculty, which accepted only one of every eight applicants in 1965, is the most popular MGU division. In the humanities, philology and journalism lead the way, with economics gaining prestige. The Juridical Faculty is apparently one of the least popular because Soviet law graduates do not inherit the earth as

American lawyers do. It is the engineers who run the big economic enterprises and hold high state and Party posts; and it is the scientists, artists, professors, and even coal miners who earned the biggest salaries. It is also bruited about that those engaged in law are affected more by changes in the Party line than are scientists and engineers.

I was unaware of all these subtleties when I arrived at the Faculty for my first appointment with my adviser. The small lobby was crowded with students hurrying to the *stolovaia* to grab lunch before classes resumed. I left my coat in the cloakroom, since it is considered *nekul'turno*—uncultured—to be found upstairs in a coat; and passing posters which announced meetings, dissertation defenses, and intramural sports events, I climbed to the second floor. There I looked into a big hall with a circular balcony, which was the Faculty's main auditorium. I wondered whether in some pre-Revolutionary incarnation the hall had been an elegant ballroom. Next I peeked into a small but impressive library, and finally I reached my destination, which was the headquarters of the *Kafedra* of Administrative and Financial Law.

At least I thought this little room, with its three tables arranged end to end, was just the *kafedra's* headquarters. Later I learned that the chamber was the seminar room, office of the head of the *kafedra* and all five assistant professors, and the *kafedra* library, too. Cramped? Of course, but at least the arrangement gave everyone a chance to listen in on Soviet-American conversations between me and my adviser. We would sit at the end of the table while his colleagues occupied all the other seats, ostensibly working at their own affairs. Often when I looked up, however, I caught them *in flagrante delicto,* and they quickly averted their eyes. The *laborantka* or secretary of the *kafedra* sat at a desk in the corner and she listened, too, until the novelty of having an American around wore off.

At my first conference with my adviser we discussed my

plan. Like Soviet factories, Soviet graduate students have a plan, which sets out month by month the work they have undertaken to accomplish. I brought in a set of proposals. I wanted to study Soviet city government and in particular the participation of voluntary groups in city affairs. I would spend a lot of time in libraries, but I requested interviews with scholars and city officials and a trip to study a provincial city in some depth. Since my goal was research, I was not expected to take courses or exams. My adviser accepted most of my proposals and arranged them in a monthly schedule. In addition, he suggested that I report to him every month on my progress, brief the entire *kafedra* on my work, and deliver a formal report on American city government to the *kafedra* at the end of the year. He invited me to attend all formal *kafedra* meetings.

How shall I sum up my year of study? I had ample cause for satisfaction and annoyance.

I had several interviews with city officials and scholars. We talked a long time (sometimes at a long green-felt-covered table with bottles of lemonade at hand), and the Russians tried to be helpful. But sometimes we had trouble communicating, and the problem wasn't language. We could converse fluently in Russian about the mechanics of Soviet public administration; but when I asked about conflict among political groups in Soviet cities, most Russians assured me there were no conflicts worth mentioning. They preferred to discourse instead on the nation's complete harmony. But even a dull interview was tolerable because I wondered whether the Russian was dull himself or simply playing it safe like petty bureaucrats everywhere. Only once, in fact, did I really suffer through an interview; and that was my own fault. Because it was a bitter cold day I had worn long underwear which was indispensable when I was out of doors but became torture when I had to sit in a hot room for two hours. May I offer a bit of advice to future American scholars in the Soviet Union? Wear long underwear at short interviews and vice versa.

Since it was impossible for an American to gain access to archives of local government units, I worked mainly in libraries. Lenin Library is a vast storehouse containing copies of all books published in the U.S.S.R. All exchange students, including Americans, had the privilege of using *Zal* Number 1, the reading room reserved for Soviet scholars holding the high ranks of Doctor and *Akademik*. That was a very useful privilege, since readers sometimes had to wait in line in the lobby for more than an hour to gain admittance to other more crowded rooms.

In the library I read *kandidat* and doctoral dissertations and found them illuminating and frustrating. The biggest problem was that Soviet scholars played down the influence of city Party committees on city governments. There were dissertations specifically devoted to the Party's role in city administration; but when I asked for permission to read them, I got a curt *"niet."*

"To read dissertations on the Party, you must be a member of the Party," I was told, "and you wouldn't want that to happen, now, would you?"

"Of course you should be able to read them," a Soviet student said, rather annoyed when I told him of the rebuff. "There's nothing to hide, since we don't make any secret of the Party's guiding role in government. You can look it up in the Party Program and the Party Rules."

"Sure, you can look it up," said a more cynical undergraduate. "The Party is supposed to guide local administration. But what would you say if you found some local Party committee runs the whole operation in detail day by day?"

Officials at one important bureau were more accommodating. They freely and graciously permitted me to read governmental decrees which are not circulated widely outside the Soviet Union. The microfilm division of Lenin Library copied for me and my American colleagues books which are not available in American libraries. And several scholars presented me with rare books from their own libraries. One man was matchless generosity itself. "Take anything you want from my bookcase," he said.

But for every obliging official there was a cringing one. I wanted to attend a meeting of the City or Borough Council or, if that was impossible, to read the minutes of such a meeting. When a high official of Moscow city government told me that the public was welcome at Borough Council meetings, I asked whether I could be invited. "We will invite you; we will indeed," he said. But every time I asked for permission to attend a specific session, I was politely informed it would be inconvenient. When I asked to see the minutes, I was not turned down flatly. I was told, "Yes, but." That is, yes, but I would have to go through channels from MGU to the Ministry of Education to the city administration. This would mean a long involved process, I was told, and I wouldn't want to go through it all, would I? I would. Well, in that case, you ought to be told that the Vietnamese war might interfere. How would I feel if I arrived to read the minutes, only to find that the staff had gone off to an anti-American rally? This was the only time the war in Vietnam was ever used as reason to block a request I made in connection with my work. But was it the real reason? "If they don't want you to see the minutes for any political reason, they might as well blame it on the war," a Soviet friend commented. In short, I never saw the minutes.

I had intended to spend two weeks at the Irkutsk University Juridical Faculty studying municipal government in that Siberian city. But after a month of planning in which my adviser, the MGU Juridical Faculty, the MGU Foreign Department, and even the Irkutsk Juridical Faculty had apparently approved the trip, the whole thing was called off. "Why?" I asked. The official explanation was that correspondence course students were coming to Irkutsk to take exams, so there would be no time for me. But the same man who told me that shrugged his shoulders and added, "Your government does it to our students. Somebody on top gets scared and makes a decision. Even if it's foolish, you can't do anything about it."

Several officials at MGU seemed genuinely distressed about the cancellation, and so did a man I telephoned at the Ministry of Higher Education. He promised to investigate the situation and asked me to call back in ten days.

"How are things going?" he asked when I called back. And as we chatted about the weather, I had the feeling he was not going to mention Irkutsk at all. Finally I asked about it. "Oh, I'm terribly sorry," he said. "It slipped my mind; the press of daily affairs, you know. Now what else was it you wanted to know?"

What explains the obstacles put in my way? How many times did a frightened literal-minded bureaucrat refuse to make a flexible interpretation of a rule which a higher authority might have allowed? How many times was the trouble only human and not political at all?

"Everything here is political, and nothing is human," a member of the American Embassy in Moscow remarked; and perhaps that is true in dealings with the Soviet Foreign Ministry. But at my level of contact with the Russians, where the stakes were lower, I wasn't so sure. I had enough experience with bungling bureaucrats to guess that not all the mix-ups were political. In the United States I have seen Soviet scholars at Harvard and Columbia involved in similar misunderstandings. They charge that they are barred from some factories and laboratories for security reasons (but not, I would guess, from city council meetings). But I have also seen Russians interpret what I knew to be innocent snafus as acts of political hostility.

There can be no denying that some of the rebuffs I

received were political. From the Soviet point of view, were they sensible?

"No bourgeois scholar can truly be objective," one senior Soviet law professor told me. "Even if you try to tell the truth, you will fall victim to the prejudices of your upbringing and the pressures from your peers. You will not be able to tell the truth about us in America. You will have to criticize us."

"Sure the authorities are cautious," said a Soviet law student quite cheerfully. "And if you think about it, you'll agree they're right. Most of our city councils do good work, but there's also plenty to criticize if that's what you want to do. I think there are good reasons for the weaknesses; we began in 1917 with virtually nothing, and remember what we lost in the Civil War and the world wars. Many of our cadres are inexperienced and funds are limited. Maybe you'll present the problem in historical perspective, but there's a good chance you won't. Maybe you're objective, but do you think the bureaucrat who makes the decision is going to risk his reputation for you?"

Other Russians disagreed. "We're wrong to deny you access to something like a city council meeting," said a professor who had connections with the Party Central Committee. "A military base is one thing—that's a security matter. But this kind of petty concealment just makes things worse. When they say you can't see something, you begin to imagine all kinds of horrors which don't in fact exist. We'd be smarter to admit our weaknesses and show you how we're trying to improve. You Americans do that all the time, and it's a smart approach. It makes a good impression on people."

It does indeed, and that's why what I saw of everyday life at the Faculty made a good impression on me. For to a remarkable extent the faculty treated me as one of its own, inviting me to participate in student activities and letting me see all sides of Faculty life: the praiseworthy, the unflattering, and the routine.

The everyday routine was not unfamiliar. *Kafedra* meetings have no parallel at Harvard or Columbia. The MGU professors discuss each other's writing as well as academic and administrative business, while graduate students listen in. But in other repects I felt at home. Soviet professors promised to speak for five minutes and held forth for twenty. They apologized for liking things. They ridiculed all journalism, including Soviet journalism, as superficial. They grumbled when it came time to write chapters for the *kafedra's* collective textbook. They complained that heavy teaching loads left little time for research and writing. And as for pressure to publish, it begins there even earlier than in America. A Soviet graduate student must publish extracts from his dissertation before he can defend it.

A Soviet professor who had visited America thought Russian scholars enjoy more prestige in Russia than Americans do in the U.S.A. He noted that Soviet professors are very well paid by Soviet standards, that a man of medium rank earned three hundred rubles a month, which is more than most physicians get and way above the average—for factory and office workers—of ninety-nine rubles. Another assistant professor said he had grown up in a poor peasant family; now he was worried that his young son would take the family's "wealth" for granted.

Some problems of Soviet scholars are peculiar to Soviet society. A woman in her thirties was just finishing a *kandidat* dissertation on the administration of justice which she had begun in 1955. Constant changes in the legal system had caused the delay. A graduate student had rewritten his thesis on municipal government four times to keep up with changes wrought by the mercurial Khrushchev. An anecdote, no doubt apocryphal, was making the rounds among Soviet students. Its hero was a scholar who had written a dissertation on Stalin's agricultural policy and in 1953 stood straining like a greyhound in the slips, ready to defend it. But then Stalin died, and the scholar had to revise his manuscript. Three years later he was ready again, when Khrushchev changed the Party line at the Twentieth Party Congress. Twice burned, the writer waited eight years before preparing his new draft, a hymn to Khrushchev's agricultural genius, just in time for Khrushchev's fall.

Student academic routine was also familiar to me. When there were no exams in sight, they worked moderately hard, but toward the end of the semester the libraries were really jammed. There were plenty of pranksters, although many of the students were in their middle twenties. Sitting in the Faculty library one day, I couldn't help eavesdropping on students in the next room who were playing with a tape recorder between periods of a criminology lecture. *"Achtung! Achtung!"* someone shouted, and suddenly everyone was imitating the whine of falling bombs. In the dorm some residents played a wild hide-and-seek game called *kobois i indeitsy* (cowboys and Indians), and one Soviet army veteran earned his nickname of Otto von Lauerbach by goose-stepping up and down the hall, stopping now and then to shout *"Seig Heil!"*

The exams took about twenty minutes, and they were oral. The student received a list of seventy questions in advance and on the day of the exam he was given two at random to answer. When I attended as an observer, the student being tested watched his professor nervously for signs and portents. The students waiting in the room to go next scribbled outlines for their answers. And outside the room, other students paced up and down telling each other how tense they were or weren't. One man pulled a table over to the door, stood on it to look over the transom, and gave his colleagues a blow-by-blow account of the proceedings:

"Sasha's in trouble. He's stalling for time. My God, am I nervous."

"Some of you don't work hard enough," a professor admonished students at a meeting. The students, who had been invited to air their gripes and grievances, had complained of a lack of key books in the library and charged that no one had taught them how to use the reference room. The professors replied that some students seemed too lazy to use the books anyway, that if a man hadn't learned to use a reference room in four years there was little hope for him, and that attendance and grades were dangerously low, especially in the evening classes.

I was surprised to hear the complaints because the students seemed to me to work hard enough and they certainly performed well in the *kruzhki,* or extracurricular study circles, which I often attended. I was invited to take part in the discussions, and once, when the topic was "The Law of Purchase and Sale in America," I was asked to comment at some length. Since the student speaker knew as much or more than I did about the subject, I related a personal anecdote. I recalled that my father had once deputized me to accept a new car in his name while he was out of town, and that I had paid and taken delivery though a clause was added by the dealer without my father's knowledge. I made it clear that my father had been very angry with me. The Soviet students seemed more interested in the family dispute than in legalities. "So you Americans have a conflict of generations, too," someone said.

Was there a conflict of Soviet generations? Students at the Juridical Faculty criticized some professors for being old-fashioned, for producing "political propaganda" rather than serious scholarship. The critics demanded what they called "a more scientific systematic approach." They called for more concrete sociological research and they were eager to use the techniques of *kibernetiki*—cybernetics. They wanted to read

American books about political pressure groups, public opinion, and business administration. They were willing to test concepts of American political science and sociology in the study of Soviet society.

The critics spoke of sociology as the most objective way to study society, as the opposite of propaganda. They recalled that Soviet sociology flourished in the twenties and then was proscribed by Stalin, who feared that its practitioners would point out the gap between theory and reality. Sociology was reborn after 1956, and since then sociological laboratories and study groups have been organized throughout the U.S.S.R. The students knew that MGU had a sociological laboratory in its Philosophy Faculty, and that the Institute of State and Law of the Academy of Science was carrying out some concrete studies of crime and of public administration. But the Juridical Faculty, the critics complained, was clinging to old ways.

A few professors sympathized with the critical students' point of view. They didn't attack their colleagues, at least when I was around, but they welcomed the new research methods, tried to be more "systematic" in their own work, and regretted that teaching obligations prevented them from doing more intensive scholarly work.

But other professors were unconvinced. They scoffed at a conference at the Academy of Sciences at which sociologists, jurists, and economists endorsed the *nauka upravleniia* or science of administration. The conference had accepted the proposition that bureaucracies in capitalist and Communist countries share similar problems, and suggested more Soviet research in the field. "Words, words, words," was one law professor's reaction. "Nothing but empty words. Our sociologists talk a lot, but what have they produced? They say they are scientific, but I'm still waiting to see the fruits of their science. We don't need any Kinsey reports in our country."

When I reported to my *kafedra* on political groups in

American cities I had a warm reception as long as I described the way they worked. But when I suggested that some American groups reminded me of Soviet organizations, a few Russians looked a little embarrassed; and one scholar took the trouble to remind everyone that the Soviet Union was a socialist country which had banished "exploitation of man by man," while the United States was not.

A Sociology Club was founded at the Juridical Faculty and an expert on historical materialism from the Philosophy Faculty addressed the first meeting.

"We have made mistakes in the past," he said. "And many scholars are still behind the times. Some people are still writing what amounts to political propaganda. We must be more scientific, and fortunately we have Marxism-Leninism to guide us. Sociology in America is a tool in the hands of business, and it degenerates into jargon that no one can understand. For us sociology is historical materialism in action. Our task is to generalize the experience of building socialism."

I expected extensive student support for the new club. But only a few people attended the founding meeting, and I never heard of a second gathering. Were the students apathetic? I have no doubt many were. But others, I think, were cynical.

"Is it really correct to say that sociology is historical materialism in action?" one student asked skeptically. "If we set out to find general laws of socialist construction, then are we really being scientific? Perhaps we will find fewer general laws than we think. We really should begin with an open mind."

"The trouble with concrete sociological research is that it is too revealing for its own good," said another skeptic. "It may reveal unflattering things about us. Take crime, for instance. We've always said that crime in the Soviet Union is a remnant of the capitalist order. But we don't publish any absolute statistics about crime. Let's suppose they launch a massive sociological study of the causes of crime. Maybe they'd find out that while the crime rate may be falling, the absolute figures are shockingly high. And maybe they'd conclude that a lot of crime is a product of Soviet conditions. If so, that's really nothing to be ashamed of. No system is perfect, and everyone knows life hasn't been so easy because of our country's backwardness and the wars. It would even be a healthy thing to know that crime is caused by Soviet conditions. After all, it helps to be realistic about the causes of crime when you're trying to eliminate it. That stands to reason. But you can bet some people on top won't see it that way. And until they do see it that way, our sociologists will have to compromise."

Whatever the division of Soviet opinion about American books on politics and sociology, I would say that all Soviet students and professors would have liked to read more American magazines and newspapers, especially *The New York Times*. One or two Russians denied that, out of pride, I suppose. And some of them would surely have found things to ridicule. But for those who studied American government and law, the lack of *The Times* was a serious matter. Said one such student, "As things are now we can't buy it on the street, we can't subscribe to it, and we need permission to read it in the library. Even the professors who specialize on America must read it in the library, and that's damn inconvenient."

I knew that some American books and newspapers were hard for Russians to get, but I was really shocked when an undergraduate who was studying the American Congress Today told me that one of his principal sources was a book by Woodrow Wilson in Russian translation. Didn't he have access to anything more contemporary? However, another student, whom I trusted, told me that the case was not typical. "We may not have as many books as we need," he said, "but we're not that badly off. The fellow reading Woodrow Wilson is just a lazy *durak* (idiot)! He probably grabbed the first book he saw on the shelf. That kind of guy will never accomplish anything."

Where do MGU students go when they graduate? Even as they finish their studies, they know that they will take a job assigned by the state and hold it for at least three years. That is how students repay the state for their free education. I had the impression that the best in physics could name their own ticket. In the Juridical Faculty, the preferences of the best got special consideration. But although all students' wishes are registered in advance, there are always unpopular places to be filled.

When the *raspredelenie*—distribution—approaches, everyone talks about his fate. Moscow is Mecca for many, and if they can't get Moscow they hope for some other big city. A good climate is important—a small city in the south may be preferable to a big city in the far north—but so is a place with theaters and concerts and museums. Students worry about salary, about the housing that comes with the job—a private apartment is preferable to a dorm room—and about prospects for moving to a better job. At the Juridical Faculty, the man or woman who becomes a judge is to be envied, although some students complain that Party membership counts more than good grades in getting a judicial post. A position in the prosecutor's office is attractive—unless that office is near the Arctic Circle. Work in the militia (police force) pays well—but you may be on your feet outdoors much of the time. And a slot in the social security system, doling out pensions, is, by all accounts, the last place most law graduates want to be—except that you may have a better chance to stay in Moscow if you work in the social security system.

I attended a meeting at the Faculty at which representatives of the State Prosecutor's Office and the social security system briefed students. The prosecutor was cheerful and relaxed. He even told anecdotes: about the two graduates who refused to serve in "the wilds of Kazakhstan" because that would be a waste of their MGU education; and about the MGU-trained prosecutor who illegally jailed the husband of his mistress. The man from social security was more sober, even grim. He tried hard to inspire his listeners to serve the aged, and he lamented the fact that MGU's Juridical Faculty offered no special courses on the law and administration of social security.

Some MGU students, the elite of the Soviet Union, seemed less idealistic than many Americans. I met virtually no one to correspond to the young Americans who volunteer to help the poor and the aged, abroad as well as at home. But on the other hand, most Soviet students were basically cheerful and ready to serve their country wherever they were sent. Some griped, but most acknowledged their prejudices and laughed at themselves. "Siberia is far enough from Moscow," one student who was being sent there consoled himself. "*Slava Bogu!* Thank God the Tsar sold Alaska."

6

Who's for *Pravda?*

"DOLOI AMERIKANSKII IMPERIALIZM! DOLOI! DOLOI! DOLOI!" chanted the Vietnamese, Chinese, and Japanese students who had jumped to their feet and were jabbing their fists in the air.

"Down with American Imperialism!" I was at an MGU rally called to support the National Liberation Front of South Vietnam and to condemn "American aggression." Red and white banners proclaiming "Solidarity with Our Vietnamese Brothers" decorated the hall. On the stage sat two rows of speakers, students from various countries. Among the thousand in the hall were Russians, Vietnamese, Chinese, Japanese, East Europeans, Africans, and Latin Americans.

I had come to the meeting after seeing photographs of "American atrocities," which the Vietnamese had posted on ten bulletin boards in the lobby. One picture purported to show a Marine executing a Vietnamese woman while her hands were tied behind her back; another had torn bodies of children "killed in an American air attack." I had seen Russians quietly examining the gruesome exhibit, but I couldn't judge their reaction.

At the rally, an MGU administrator spoke first. He lauded

the Vietnamese people at length and attacked America. Russians in the audience applauded. The Vietnamese applauded. But the Chinese, sitting apart, sat immobile. A Vietnamese thanked both the U.S.S.R. and China for their aid and got a standing ovation from everyone. A young man introduced as the head of the Chinese delegation tore into America mercilessly, as if to show the Russians how to do it. The Vietnamese cheered, but Russians applauded less enthusiastically. The speakers from East Europe were restrained, echoing the Russians. A Cuban vowed support until "victory or death" (of the Vietnamese, I presumed). While a Japanese spoke, his compatriots chanted in unison the Russian phrase *"Doloi Amerikanskii Imperializm,"* and spelled out the slogan with cards, like fans at an American college football game.

From time to time, Chinese, Vietnamese, and Japanese students leaped up like cheerleaders and screamed *"Doloi! Doloi! Doloi!"* I had entered the hall unnoticed, but when these outbursts erupted, I feared that I would be the only one to remain seated. I needn't have worried. As far as I could see, not one Russian jumped up to join the angry chorus. In fact, the Russians sitting near me seemed positively detached. Some sat reading books, while others gossiped. They applauded perfunctorily, it seemed to me, except on special occasions. They cheered a Soviet professor, but apparently only because he was *their* professor and hence a native son. When an MGU Party official spoke, they laughed and clapped at his sputtering delivery, obviously a familiar failing of his. They cheered most loudly for a classmate, who delivered a passionate tirade and ended by shouting, *"Yanki von, von, von iz Vietnam* (Yankee, go home, home, home from Vietnam)." But the cheering was more raucous than respectful, reminding me of Harvard students sarcastically hailing the good guys in bad Westerns. As if to confirm my suspicion that the orator was getting a razzing from his peers, one of them murmured in mockery, "My God! Look what our quiet class has given birth to."

Throughout the two-hour meeting, Soviet photographers and movie cameramen prowled the aisles shooting scenes of outraged studentry, particularly, it seemed, mixed groups from Asia, Africa, and Europe. I shrank in my seat when the cameramen passed, and I was relieved when the lights went out for a movie on Vietnam. I expected to see more horrible scenes of war, but the film depicted a North Vietnamese delegation's tour of the Soviet Union. Russians near me got up to leave. "Who needs a travelogue?" one of them wanted to know. "Now we'll just hear more speeches. A little blood would have been more realistic."

The rally, which took place early in my stay at MGU, raised more questions than it answered. What did the Russians think of the screaming Asians? Were they merely amused or truly annoyed by their demagogic classmate? Were they tired of slogans, placards, and speeches, or did they think them justified by the pictures on the bulletin boards? I didn't know. Early in the year they preferred to discuss the weather, their studies, and comparisons of Russian and American customs, clothes, and prices.

In the months I was getting to know the Russians and they were getting to trust me, almost everyone was cautious. I felt like an outsider, and I spent more time than I wanted to contemplating propaganda placards, reading *Pravda* and listening to Moscow Radio. That was a little depressing, but it was useful preparation for the time when I began to realize that I was paying more attention to placards, *Pravda,* and Moscow Radio than most of the Russians around me. It was only then that I knew I was beginning to grasp the subtle differences within the university in general and the Juridical Faculty in particular.

The propaganda displays fascinated me; they offered an absorbing parade of state-managed hyperbole. "Lenin Lived.

Lenin Lives. Lenin Will Live," declared the huge red billboard on Leninskii Prospekt. *"Slava Kommunisticheskoi Partii Sovetskogo Soiuza* (Glory to the Communist Party of the Soviet Union) " proclaimed a glaring neon display which, on Times Square, might have been blowing giant smoke rings. *"My s toboi Partiia* (We're with You, Party) " vowed the red banners stretched across streets to honor the anniversary of the *"Velikaia Oktiabr'skaia Sotsialisticheskaia Revoliutsiia* (Great October Socialist Revolution) ."

I subscribed to *Pravda* and it was delivered to my door every morning. My *sosed,* who got up before I did, read it first—"I'm just censoring it," he said—and then slid it under my door to the edge of my bed. I could read *Pravda* without getting up; but sometimes after I read the undiluted accounts of American treachery in Asia, American depravity at home, and the triumphs of Communism in Outer Mongolia, I didn't feel like getting out of bed.

My room had a one-channel *priomnik*—radio receiver—which picked up the First Program of Moscow Radio. I heard some Mozart and Shostakovitch on it, but there was also a monotonous succession of thin dull stuff played at the request of *kolkhozniks*—collective farmers—not much higher in quality, I suspect, than the hillbilly tunes broadcast endlessly in some parts of the American hinterlands. Moscow Radio also went in for super-cheerful hosts (and hostesses, too), who reminded me of the most unctuous American disk jockeys. The news was brought to you by teams of announcers, one male and one female, who took turns reading bulletins, in chummy sugary and exuberant tones when reporting how Soviet miners had overfulfilled their Plans, but turning stern and somber when discussing American foreign policy. There were poems read in response to requests from Old Bolsheviks, including a rhymed hymn to Lenin and turbines; and then there were interviews with Old Bolsheviks who condemned new poets who didn't sing enough of Lenin and turbines. I heard John Lewis and the Modern Jazz Quartet late one evening—was it programed late for the same reason that American networks delay some shows until children have gone to bed?—but another night I heard *"Schastlivchik* Teddy (Happy Teddy)," a soap opera about money grubbing behind the scenes of American jazz.

What a tender tale it was! How my heart palpitated at its emotionalism. How touching that the Soviet radio cared so much about an exploited American and was willing to shed such indignant tears over him. I cannot forbear to summarize this gem of Soviet art.

Teddy Silver, the saxophone player, and his brother Dan are flying home from Europe with the members of Dan's band. Blending with the muffled roar of the plane's motors and the tinkling of cocktail glasses is music: Glenn Miller's "Moonlight Serenade" and Dean Martin crooning "C'est Si Bon." Suddenly the music stops. The plane is going down, crash-landing somewhere over the dark Atlantic. Now we are in New York Hospital with Teddy apparently the lone survivor. Miraculously he has escaped serious injury. A man enters, an unscrupulous jazz impresario, who has bribed his way past the doctor with a crisp hundred-dollar bill. He is threatening Teddy, who owes him money: Play tonight at the Palace or go to jail. "Introducing Teddy Silver," the M.C. at the theater is saying. "Happy, Happy Teddy, who forgot his parachute but not his saxophone." The crowd loves it. And Teddy, expressing his heartbreak for his brother and his band, plays as he has never played before. Even the promoter's hard-boiled girl friend is touched. "How can he play that way? Why did he leave the hospital?" she asks. "That's the way it is," the promoter replies. "That's the way it is."

How did the Russians respond to the pervasive Party line? Were they buying it, or was it just part of the landscape? A meeting observing the anniversary of the Revolution at the

Philological Faculty gave me a clue. The evening consisted of three parts, a *torzhestzennaia chast'*—ceremonial section—a concert of student turns, and dancing. The scene during the *torzhestvennaia chast'* was familiar; a hall filled with students, ten professors sitting as a presidium on the stage, and red banners overhead. "We have greatly increased our production of aluminum, steel, and assorted heavy industrial products in the last ten years," droned a professor of literature without looking up from his text. In the audience young men busily introduced themselves to young ladies, girls whispered among themselves and other students casually strolled in and out of the hall. I expected the chairman to call for order, since the audience's manners seemed shocking to me. But apparently I was in the minority. The dignitaries on the platform looked bored, and everyone seemed relieved when the speechmaking was over.

When the dancing began the students suddenly came alive. The first number was a waltz, which they did respectably but perfunctorily. But after that there were only twists and frugs and a bunny hop or two, and I quickly found myself out-twisted and out-frugged.

If I was one of the few at the dance who didn't really swing, I was also one of the rare students who read *Pravda* fully and faithfully every day. I could hardly believe this strange truth, since *Pravda* is the voice of the Party Central Committee, and its daily four to six pages are supposed to be national gospel. At MGU you can tell what paper a man subscribes to because it sticks out of his mailbox, but *Pravda* was rarely visible. I checked the university newsstands every day and decided that if I had five kopecks for every unsold *Pravda* and five for every sold *Vechernaia Moskva—Evening Moscow*—I would be rich. For copies of *Pravda* had to be carried away at the end of the day, while "*Vechiorka,*" as the evening paper is affectionately nicknamed by Muscovites, sold out almost immediately. *Vechiorka* is a lively paper with brief stories of local interest and a back page full of movie ads and announcements of job openings, lectures, and dissertation defences open to the public. Until the divorce reform of 1965, *Vechiorka* also carried announcements of divorces, which the law required couples have published. "How can I find a copy of *Vechernaia Moskva?*" I asked a Russian after failing many times to find it on the stands. "Just find the longest line and get on it," he said. I did so one afternoon at four; and when I reached the kiosk window, I was handed a copy of *Vechiorka* without even asking.

I had the impression that Russians at least skimmed through *Pravda*—which was available in dormitory lounges—to get the main news of the day, and law students read it to keep up with official announcements. But when I read an interesting article in *Pravda* and told my friends about it, they usually hadn't read it and asked to borrow my copy. *Izvestia* (*News*), which is the organ of the Soviet government and as authoritative as *Pravda,* seemed to be more popular—"Because it's more factual," one Russian said—and so was the lively *Komsomolskaia Pravda,* the voice of the Young Communist League. *Novy Mir* (*New World*) and *Iunost* (*Youth*), the two literary magazines which were attacked by Party conservatives in 1966, sold out shortly after they hit the stands, and old issues were passed from hand to hand in the dormitory. But the more conservative literary journals like *Oktiabr* (*October*) and *Neva* were always available. *Innostrannaia Literatura* (*Foreign Literature*), which in 1966 printed translations of Ionesco's *Rhinoceros* and Capote's *In Cold Blood,* was perhaps the most popular publication of all. As far as I could see, it wasn't sold at news kiosks, and a friend with a subscription to it was a friend indeed. *Nauka i Zhizn* (*Science and Life*) was read by many nonscientists who welcomed it as a lively, objective journal unencumbered by politics and ideology.

The choice of Western newspapers on Moscow newsstands

was limited, but students seized what there was. They rushed down in the morning to get the British Communist Party's *Daily Worker* (now called *The Morning Star*), the French Party's *L'Humanité,* and the Italian Party's *L'Unità.* They bought papers from Poland, Czechoslovakia, and East Germany. Reading them was good language practice, but it was also good reading. *The Morning Star* resembles the *London Evening Standard* more than *Pravda,* and it makes Soviet papers look stodgy. This was the paper that first informed Soviet students that Western Communists had condemned the trial of Andrei Sinyavsky and Yuli Daniel, the writers accused of slandering the Soviet Union in works published in the West. During the course of the trial, copies of *The Star* and *L'Humanité* were gobbled up immediately. Students I knew had no illusion that the American *Worker* or *The Morning Star* had massive popular followings in America and Britain. They read them because there was nothing else available, except perhaps *Za Rubezhom* (*Abroad*), a Soviet magazine which reprints a surprisingly broad range of articles from the Western press.

I obtained my most cogent piece of evidence about newspaper circulation quite accidentally at the Subscriptions Office in the basement of MGU. I was about to subscribe to several Soviet publications when I was interrupted by a smiling individual who looked like a Fuller Brush man. He was making an official survey of MGU reading habits and he began to look grim as the clerk read numbers from a complicated graph. I didn't pay much attention until the pollster threw up his hands and cried, "Isn't this a shame! Isn't this a disgrace! Only a handful of subscriptions to *Pravda* in the whole place."

Later I mentioned this phenomenon to a Soviet friend, adding that *Pravda* deserved its low esteem. "Of course it does," he said, "but don't leap to the wrong conclusions. *Pravda* is a dull, pompous paper full of propaganda, and you must read our more serious journals to get a more objective view. But that doesn't mean that Soviet people don't believe a lot of what's printed in *Pravda.* They simply don't like to wade through all of it every day. It's as if you had to read a Fourth of July oration every morning. You'd be bored, but you'd accept most of it."

Students I knew usually ignored the news broadcasts to which I listened on my *priomnik.* They chose to listen instead to music, including Western jazz and folk music taped from foreign radio broadcasts and from records that circulated in the dorm. I was subjected to more of the Beatles' music in Moscow than I ever heard in the U.S., or did it just seem that way because the selection of records was smaller and they kept playing the same songs over and over? The sound of other Westerners came through the floor and walls, too. I fell asleep to Nat "King" Cole and the Weavers more times than I care to recall.

I was surprised when a Russian ran into my room to tell me about the Gemini 6 flight, which had not been mentioned on a Soviet news broadcast. *"Golos Ameriki* (Voice of America)," he said when I asked the source of his information. He had been listening on a shortwave set while sitting with friends at the phone desk, and the group had delegated him to congratulate me, he grinned, and through me the American people.

Moscow Radio did eventually cover the Gemini flights, but I learned from Soviet friends with shortwave sets about the Soviet intellectuals who petitioned the Central Committee to oppose rehabilitation of Stalin and to defend Sinyavsky and Daniel. I was amazed how freely and fearlessly students listened to and quoted *Golos Ameriki,* for I had thought it even might be embarrassing for an American to listen.

"Our government used to jam *Golos Ameriki,*" a Soviet friend explained. "But even then people listened. In those days the test of a good shortwave radio was whether it could pick up *Golos Ameriki*. People used to test a set that way before they bought it. Nowadays, with *Golos Ameriki* coming in loud and clear, we've got no way of knowing."

Did Soviet students respect *Golos Ameriki* for reporting criticism of America? Or did they take that as a sign of weakness? Later in the year I asked about that.

"Weakness?" the Russian repeated incredulously. "Have you forgotten your own propaganda? That's what America is all about, I thought. You know, free speech, everyone can criticize the President, and all the rest. That's what people expect from *Golos Ameriki*. Now, your Radio Liberty is something else again. The trouble with Radio Liberty is that it attacks us too crudely, and that's a bore. If we want to hear crude attacks, they're much more fun on Radio Peking."

I heard Radio Peking one evening as I passed the phone desk in the dorm. Several Russians lounging there were listening to somebody's short wave set. "The Khrushchevist revisionist clique of so-called Soviet leaders is plotting to restore capitalism in the U.S.S.R. and helping American imperialism to enslave the Vietnamese people," intoned the Chinese Radio's Russian language service. One of the Russians at the desk muttered angrily that the charges were ludicrous, but others guffawed. "If that's the way they feel, let's listen to our so-called allies on *Goros Ameliki*," said one grinning Russian, switching l's and r's, slanting his eyes with his hands, and bringing down the house.

7

Oracle at the *Punkt*

On the day of my first *dezhurstvo* I was somewhat apprehensive when I crawled out of bed shortly after 7:00 A.M. I had heard about *dezhurstvo.* The word means duty, and it summed up the housekeeping chores at which each student took a turn each month: sweeping the halls, mopping the kitchen, and answering the telephones at the *punkt* —point—near the lounge. What would *dezhurstvo* be like? Would I be given the same assignments as everyone else? I hoped so, for, as I had told a Soviet friend, I was ready and willing to serve my stint.

"Are you crazy or something?" my friend had replied. "Cleaning up is dirty work and answering the phones is a bore. You should be grateful if they let you off."

The brutal truth, which in my innocence I did not know at the time of my first *dezhurstvo,* was that some Russians went to ingenious lengths to goof off. On *dezhurstvo* eve, these characters would take refuge in a friend's *blok* and spend the night in it, sometimes even sleeping on the floor. Then, when the *kommandantsha* came to summon them to the broom and the mop, they were not in. "Kolia's already gone to class," Kolia's well-rehearsed *sosed* would inform the *kommandantsha* while Kolia slept peacefully a few *bloks* away.

When students pulled tricks like that, the kitchen remained dirty, and no one answered the phones for hours at a time. That, however, was their business (students on other floors seemed to be more conscientious). I was determined to show that an American could abide by the rules.

"Well, at least pick Sunday for your *dezhurstvo*," my friend had urged. "The *kommandantsha* doesn't come in on Sundays and neither do the cleaning ladies. That means there's no one to check that you've cleaned the kitchen. Furthermore, people sit around the phone desk at the *punkt* gossiping on Sunday, so they can answer their own calls and you can skip that, too."

Perhaps I was exaggerating the significance of *dezhurstvo*. I didn't want to be a shirker, but I didn't want to be known as a boy scout either. I chose Sunday.

A Russian was already at work sweeping when I emerged from my room. He grumbled something about going back to sleep and then informed me that the girl who was supposed to be the third member of the clean-up squad had left us a note: she had swept her corridor and mopped one of the kitchens before retiring the night before. "*Dobroe utro, mal'chiki* (Good morning, boys)," said her cheerful little greeting.

Since Soviet brooms, which consist of straw bound to short stubs of bamboo, are about three feet long, I felt like a giant sweeping the floor with a couple of toothpicks. But my colleague, taller than I, was having no trouble. His broom skimmed along merrily. He swept a little under a doorway, a little to the side, a little into a dust pan, and that was that. He swept the kitchen, too, instead of mopping it; but I, like a model *komsomolets* (young Communist), followed the rules. I collected the potato peelings and other loose garbage that was strewn about the floor and stuffed it down the garbage chute. Then I got out a pail of water and swabbed the floor, scrubbed the sinks, and scoured the ovens.

"Don't bother putting the morning papers on the reading table," said my Russian partner, who had been through the routine many times and was determined to get it done as quickly as possible. "Nobody does that any more. And don't worry about the phones. If you do answer them, don't bother to write down messages for people who aren't home. The message book hasn't been used in years. But you'd be smart to forget about the phones entirely. There'll be plenty of people there to answer them. You'll see."

My shift at the *punkt* ran from 7:00 P.M. to 11:00, and several students were standing around the phone desk when I arrived. I plugged in the table lamp I had brought from my room, spread out some books on the desk, and settled myself in an easy chair behind the desk. The phone rang and I picked up the receiver. What with loungers gabbing by the desk and the static on the line, I couldn't make out which *blok* the caller wanted.

"Khotite shestidesiatyi?" I asked. Did the caller want *blok* number sixty?

"Oh, that must be for Dima," said one of the Russians who was standing at the *punkt*. "It must be Liuda calling again. She never stops calling him; can't take no for an answer. Tell her nobody's home in *shestidesiatyi*."

Poor Liuda. What right did I have to transmit the brush-off, especially from someone I had never met? I decided to buzz *shestidesiatyi* so that Dima could handle the matter himself. But just then I heard again from what I thought was Liuda.

"Niet," said the voice on the phone, which now sounded too deep to belong to a female. *"Mne nuzhen shestnadsatyi."*

The caller wanted *blok* number sixteen, not sixty; and it was a he. My mistake!

"What's wrong with Liuda?" a second fellow at the desk

was saying. "She's a nice *devchonka.* Why doesn't Dima like her?"

But by this time I was already pressing a button on the desk which rang a buzzer in number sixteen. *"Idu, idu* (I'm coming)," shouted the occupant of that *blok* from somewhere in the distance, and presently he came running down the hall. There were two phones on the desk, and two extensions in private booths; but despite the noise at the *punkt,* the man from number sixteen, and most of the other people I buzzed, didn't bother to take their calls in the booth.

It was not long before a crowd assembled at the *punkt.* Callers lingered to chat. Students watching television in the lounge next door came out to rub their eyes and smoke. The elevators were around the corner, and people on their way home stopped to listen without removing coats and hats. Some men wore their Sunday best, a suit with a white shirt and tie instead of the usual dark knit shirt; but others, taking a study break, wore sport shirts and the ever-present blue sweat pants. A few girls, called to the phone, stayed to listen; and toward the end of the evening, several *studentki* appeared in bathrobes and curlers covered with kerchiefs.

"You're the *amerikanets,* aren't you?" asked a young man with a mustache when I first settled myself at the desk. Though I had never lounged through an evening at the *punkt,* I had passed by enough times to recognize the questioner as a regular.

"What kind of room did you have in your university dormitory at home?" he asked. "How much did you pay for it, and how much for food?"

When I said that room, board, and tuition added up to nearly $3,000, they were stunned.

"You mean you pay $3,000 just for the education! Why, we get it free and room and board cost practically nothing. Hey, *rebiata* (fellows), our system isn't so bad after all."

I was about to break through the hubbub to mention

American state universities and fellowships of all kinds when the mustached student interrupted me. "Take it easy, *rebiata*," he said. "First of all, don't badger him; and secondly, haven't you ignorant guys ever heard of their state universities and fellowships of all kinds? You have those in America, don't you?"

"What academic degrees does one get at an American university?"

"What are the professorial ranks?"

"How much are college teachers paid?"

After my answers, the students excitedly compared the American situation with their own.

"How much does a car cost in the States?"

Oohs and aahs at the answer.

"How much does an American pay for meat, milk, bread, a week of skiing, and a week at the beach?"

I did the best I could to give precise replies.

"Would you mind very much if I ask a more delicate question?" asked a thin, nervous young man who looked anything but athletic in his athletic sweat suit.

"Go ahead," I said; but the others looked embarrassed as he posed his question.

"Is it really true that you have great unemployment in America?" He paused, apparently to make sure that I was not annoyed. He knew these were *spornye voprosy*—controversial questions—but he couldn't resist asking them. "Is it really true that Americans treat *chiornye* (blacks) very badly?"

The Russians at the desk seemed to be holding their breath for fear that I would take offense, and they were visibly relieved when I didn't. I answered that there were several million unemployed Americans and too many guilty of bigotry and racial prejudice. But I was interrupted before I could elaborate on causes and cures for these ills.

"Now, wait a minute, Seriozha," a big burly fellow said to the thin young man. "What makes you think we don't have any unemployment? Of course we do, or if we don't, we really should have it. Look at all the *kolkhozniki* doing nothing on farms, and you watch how many unproductive workers will start losing jobs when our factories begin to worry more about profits. As for blacks, don't forget the Africans. We don't have many here, but we've got enough to make things uncomfortable."

Seriozha shot back that socialism had the heart to protect workers and their jobs, and that blacks were treated better in the U.S.S.R. than in the U.S.A. A third chap disagreed. "Let's be honest," he said. "Some of us treat Africans pretty badly, too, especially when they try to run around with Russian girls."

The questions were getting tougher, building toward really embarrassing issues. In a soft voice, a neatly dressed girl asked a question. I couldn't make it out and neither could others. "*Gromche* (louder)," someone yelled. "She wants to know who really killed President Kennedy," a boy in front called out. "She wonders whether the Warren report tells the whole story."

I assured them that I knew as little as they did. I could only state my conviction that Chief Justice Warren was a man of integrity. And I recalled that the United States has never had a conspiratorial political tradition.

The students at the desk had not read the Warren report, which, they admitted ruefully, was not available in the U.S.S.R. But they had read abstracts of critical books printed in the Soviet press, as their questions showed. How could Oswald have fired all the shots in so short a time? How had Ruby managed to gain entry into the police station? What was patrolman J. D. Tippet's connection with the crime?

A year before, Russians had asked some of the same questions. And the questions were nearly always the prelude to personal recollections. Nearly everyone remembered as vividly as I where he had been when the news of the assassination came. People of all ages had told me how deeply they were moved by the tragic fate of a man they respected and admired.

"I almost can't forgive the American people for letting President Kennedy be killed," said the girl at the *punkt* who had raised the subject, and this time she spoke loudly enough for me to hear. Everyone was silent for a moment after that.

"What kind of passport do you have to carry when you travel inside the U.S.A?" someone asked, breaking the silence.

"None," I replied, slightly stunned by the swift change of subject.

"None?" Well, you must carry some kind of identification."

"A driver's license," I explained, "or a draft card, or a university burser's card is sufficient."

"What do they look like? May we see them?"

At first I was puzzled by the line of questioning, but I extracted the cards in question from my wallet and passed them around. One of the Russians appeared to be puzzled too, for he complained that this was *melochi*—trivia.

"*Tishe.* (Pipe down.) *Tishe rebiata,*" said another student who was excitedly examining my draft card. "This is the key. The card has no picture on it, and not even an official seal. That's absolutely crucial."

As they passed around the cards I remembered that Soviet citizens carry internal passports and that students' *propusks* had pictures attached, too. Although Russians no longer need official permission to switch jobs and move about the country, they do need official approval to take up residence in certain overcrowded cities.

After the students returned my cards, a somber-faced dark-haired man, who had only one arm, asked the question I had been anticipating with some nervousness. "What are you

Americans doing in Vietnam? And while you're at it, would you mind telling us why you are helping the Germans to get nuclear arms?"

By now there were nearly thirty students clustered around the *punkt,* and some of them appeared startled by the questioner's hostile tone. I was surprised too, for I suppose I had been deluding myself. The Russians' mildness at the Vietnam protest rally I had attended had misled me. I confess I had been enjoying my role as oracle at the *punkt,* but now I felt presumptuous and ill-at-ease. However, I couldn't run away from the question.

"I don't agree with everything the American government has done in Vietnam," I said. "But since I'm the only American here right now I'll tell what they think in Washington. Then if you're interested I'll tell you where I disagree."

I set forth the American Administration's position and added American concern about China's militant threats and her taunts that the U.S. is a paper tiger.

"How many Chinese are fighting in Vietnam? Just tell us that, please," said the one-armed man. "And who is guilty of aggression? Who has sent 300,000 troops, and who is bombing a small defenseless country? Everybody knows America is the strongest country in the world, and that your fleet could wipe out China itself. You only look ridiculous trying to destroy little Vietnam."

His tone was ominous and I feared that the discussion would degenerate into clichés.

"You know, you Russians are rather self-righteous," I could not resist saying. "All wars are wrong except the wars that you say are just. How can you criticize intervention in Vietnam after the way you intervened in Hungary?"

"Well, all I can say," said the Russian with a flash of a grin, "is that Hungary, at least, is right across our border, and not 10,000 kilometers away."

A couple of students snickered at this bit of realpolitik, and one whispered something about measuring morality in kilometers.

I began to think that we might be able to have a serious discussion of Vietnam after all. But someone called out that it was getting late and we hadn't discussed Germany yet.

By this time I was sprawled deep in the easy chair with my feet on the desk. Now when the phones rang, students not involved in the debate answered, paged those being called, and directed them into the private booths so as not to disturb us. Some listeners abandoned the *punkt* to get some studying done, but others replaced them. "*Kto govorit* (who's speaking) ?" the newcomers asked, and they were informed that it was "*nash amerikanskii student* (our American student)." Nobody knew that *nash amerikanskii student* by this time had a terrible *amerikanskii* headache and that he remained on the witness stand with the greatest reluctance.

I repeated a question. "Why is America going to give nuclear weapons to the Germans? Well, first of all we are not going to do so, as your government will admit when it signs a treaty to prevent the spread of nuclear weapons."

"But everybody knows," objected another Russian, "that the Pentagon is counting on a Germany with nuclear arms to threaten us. Why are you so gentle and solicitous with Germany? I'll tell you why. Because you didn't live through two world wars. Because your country didn't lose twenty million men in the last war. You Americans don't really know what war is like. If you did, you couldn't napalm the Vietnamese, and you could never dream of giving the Germans nuclear weapons."

I began to talk about the need to integrate Germany into Europe instead of isolating and infuriating her as the Allies did after the First World War. But for the Russians, the lesson of the twenties was the opposite: German capitalists and their bourgeois allies in Britain, France, and America had built up Hitler to fight Communism. After speaking so long in Russian, I found myself fumbling frantically for a phrase in English to express the complexity of the historical tangle we were discussing. I caught myself hoping that the student nicknamed Otto von Lauerbach would choose this moment to come goose-stepping down the hall, injecting a little levity into the proceedings with his familiar imitation of a German soldier. I really didn't have the energy to pursue the matter further—and fortunately I didn't have to. A Russian got me off the spot.

"Hey, didn't we once give some nuclear weapons to someone called Castro?" he said. "That wasn't very smart of us, was it?"

"We sure did," put in someone else, "but Nikita Sergeevich was smart enough to get the missiles right back."

Laughter cut the tension.

"What are you going to do about cadres this year?" a student asked me—and several others grinned.

"Cadres?" I asked innocently. "What do you mean?"

"You know, girls. Cadres means girls. That's student slang. To make a girl is *zakadrit'*."

It took me a moment to catch the pun. The word cadre is the root of the verb *"zakadrit'!"*

The Russians laughed. "Come on," one of them said. "Don't duck the issue. What do you think of our *studentki*?"

I said I thought the Soviet girls were lovely, that although they did without extensive wardrobes and wore less make-up than American girls, they looked every bit as nice as American girls, who, I assured my listeners, were also lovely.

"Hurrah," they shouted. "The man's a patriot and a diplomat too."

"Who's more curious, Russians about America, or Americans about the Soviet Union?" came the next question.

Russians I had met were more eager to learn about America, I said. The evening's discussion proved how eager.

I was stimulated but exhausted by the relentless questioning, and I was relieved when a student changed the subject again.

"You play the guitar, don't you? Could we get you to sing us some American folk songs?"

Though weary, I said I'd try. I got my guitar, an excellent instrument that I had bought for fifteen rubles in a Soviet store and which would have cost over forty dollars in the States. It was now past midnight and the phone was no longer ringing. We adjourned to the lounge. I played and sang the songs they requested: "Where Have All the Flowers Gone?," "She'll Be Coming Round the Mountain," "Clementine," and "We Shall Overcome." Then I offered to play for some Russian singing and I suggested "Moscow Nights," which has been a hit for years in Moscow.

"Oh, no," said a Russian. "That's a bore. We'll sing you some good ones."

And they did.

8

Take Me Out to the Ball Game

THE students I met at the *punkt* sang some lovely old Russian ballads and some rousing songs from the Russian Civil War. That was their idea of "good ones."

Later, as my guitar introduced me to more Russians, I heard other student favorites. Those that made the deepest impression on me were the hitherto unpublished and unrecorded songs written by prisoners in Stalin's prison camps, which I heard in student renditions and on underground tapes.

I heard over and over again the works of Bulat Okudzhava. Every Russian student I met knew the words of Okudzhava's songs; and those familiar with the American music scene referred to him as a kind of Soviet Bob Dylan, a troubadour whose words do not always echo the Party's description of the great Soviet society. Okudzhava's songs circulated on private tapes before they began to appear as recordings, and the reason for the delay seems obvious. Some of his somber songs are clearly out of tune with the Party's official optimism, and his message is almost existential; witness the last stanzas of one that I tried to memorize:

Let me live my life to the fullest,
And then let me be led
For all my deeds
To the very Last Judgment.

There is no forgiveness there
And for a whole eternity after
For all seven crimes there is only one punishment,
One answer: Nonsense.

There were also songs composed by MGU students to immortalize their faculties in earnest as well as in fun. And there was the song of the captured American U-2 pilot homesick in his Soviet cell. "San Antonio," he sings, "*kak eto po-russki? Bednaia moia mat'* (San Antonio—how is that in Russian? My poor mother.) "

But for the most part Russians were more eager to hear me sing American songs than to sing their own to me. They wanted to hear folk music and the latest hits. They asked by name for old numbers like "Only You," which the Platters sang in the dawn of rock and roll. Luckily I remembered the old songs from my adolescent days as a jazz addict. I had occasionally wondered how I could banish the useless words and music from my memory; and now, unexpectedly, I had an audience which wanted to hear them complete with falsetto "ooh wah" and deep bass "yeah, man." Four members of a Juridical Faculty jazz combo knew the music to countless songs of Jerome Kern and Rodgers and Hart and begged me to sing the words, which they didn't know. Others asked to borrow recordings of Dave Brubeck and Miles Davis, if only for the time it took to find a tape recorder and tape them. When I promised to give a girl a recording of *West Side Story* and then forgot, I received a petition from ten of her friends reminding me of my pledge.

I met a young Russian who wore American blue jeans and cowboy boots and categorically refused to listen to Russian songs. He was interested, he declared, in American folk music and particularly in the latest folk rock. He was delighted to meet an American but was disappointed when it turned out that I knew fewer Bob Dylan songs than he and could teach him no new words and chords. In fact, the only thing that saved the evening was that he could teach me new American words and chords, which he did in a patronizing way.

The Bob Dylan expert had friends who tried to be as Westernized as he. They papered the walls of their room with pictures of Western film stars, dressed in a fashionably Western way, and craved copies of American magazines. They made up a circle of men and women who often gathered to sing and talk. The spirit at those sessions was informal, as it was at all MGU parties I attended: students wandered in, ate and drank if there was vodka and sausage available, and wandered out. It was difficult to tell which couples were steady pairs, and unattached students were welcome. As an American, I was especially welcome, and one evening my hosts produced a game they said I would enjoy. It was the old American board game of Monopoly, complete with play money, properties, houses, and hotels. Another American had given them the game, and they had translated and learned the rules. They expected great things from me, they said, since I lived not far from Wall Street. But the shrewdest capitalist was a pretty Russian girl who was the banker. All I could get command of were a few railroads, and I let the girl talk me into selling them to her. I was the first to go bankrupt.

It should be made clear that this was the only game of Monopoly I saw all year, and I ran into it early in my stay. At the outset, the Russians easiest to get to know were Americaphiles. They had cultivated Americans in previous years, and they made me uneasy. I had nothing against them, but I was anxious to meet Russians who did not begin by being too flattering. The chap with the cowboy boots was unique; the vast majority of Russians wore Russian shoes. Most of the students I met were curious about American music and fond of it, but most of them were willing to sing Russian songs, too.

Two students who specialized in Russian songs asked me to teach them "The Hammer Song" and "We Shall Overcome," and proposed to perform them at a university *kontsert* in honor of the anniversary of the Revolution. The Bob Dylan expert had long since left these songs behind, but my enthusiastic pupils knew neither words nor music. Since one of the boys knew no English, he learned the words by rote. And since they couldn't find my six-string chords on their seven-string Soviet guitar, they worked out an approximate progression of sounds and labeled them numbers one, two, and three. Practice did not make perfect—just a little less bad. Eventually I sat in the audience as my students unrhythmically hammered out freedom and proclaimed, off key but enthusiastically, that they would overcome, walk hand in hand, and live in peace together. Their listeners, who had been urged earlier in the evening by a Party speaker to march on to the victory of Communism, cheered the American songs.

My Russian friends were always high-spirited and ready to have a good time. When a group of them, plus a few Americans, were escorted by one of the university's outstanding historians to the famous battlefield of Borodino, they couldn't resist breaking into song as the bus rolled through the countryside. As the scholar led us across the fields where Napoleon's and Kutuzov's armies once clashed and where cattle now graze, as we walked up and down the green redoubts, while our guide lingered over every position and enumerated every regiment in the battle, a few of my Russian colleagues drifted away to play hide-and-seek in the woods. Another whispered wistfully that he would rather see the places where Prince Andrei Bolkonsky fell and where

Pierre Bezhukhov wandered during the battle. We picnicked on the grass and afterwards several Russians threw away their empty bottles, shattering them on the hard surface of the sacred national battleground. I wasn't surprised to observe this seeming desecration, for I knew that breaking bottles was a favorite MGU pastime. In fact the sport found its most dramatic expression at the dormitory where the students blithely tossed bottles from windows as high as the nineteenth story. Was bottle-throwing an outlet for repressed aggressions? Was it a reaction against a society which demands conformity with the collective and respect for state property? Would there be less littering if young people had other ways to let off steam? I wondered about that the time I saw a six-year-old jump two feet in the air in the MGU courtyard when a bottle burst a few feet away from him. And I asked a Russian about it in the bus on the way home from Borodino. The student, a future historian, shrugged. "It's a big country with plenty of places to throw things." No one seemed interested in any serious discussion. On the way back to Moscow, we sang Russian and American folk songs.

Foreign students at MGU were as interested as Russians in American jazz and folk music. Not, apparently, the Chinese or Vietnamese or the Japanese sent by the Japanese Communist Party—I never heard them whistling "Clementine" in the hall, and they always ignored our Soviet-American hootenannies. But I sang with Congolese, Hungarians, and Cubans. And I met some Indonesians who did the swingingest rendition of "Tom Dooley" I've ever heard. When I sang a Negro spiritual for them, a lovely dark-skinned Indonesian girl asked hesitantly whether she could put a question. She was charming and intelligent and spoke several languages. "How dark is colored in America?" she asked. I was staggered by the question. I didn't know how to answer it. As I hesitated, the reason for her question became apparent as she posed another, "Would I be treated as a Negro in New York?"

Later that evening I met an effervescent Bulgarian, a scholar in his forties, who, as I later learned, never failed to pump your hand and act as if meeting you had made his day. His great aim in life was to communicate with people of all races and creeds. Although his English was miserable, he sensed the meaning of "We Shall Overcome," and when he finally grasped it all, he smiled beatifically. "Humanism, humanism," he cried exultantly, rose, and pumped my hand. Then he sat down and laboriously copied the words in Russian translation to take back to Bulgaria. Is it possible that he couldn't have found them in Bulgaria?

Sports were for me another avenue to closer contact with Soviet students. Not intercollegiate sports, for they hardly produced a ripple in the MGU routine. There were no pep rallies, no alumni reunions, no hysteria of school spirit to bring students together. But almost everyone exercised, whether by doing calisthenics to the radio's instructions, or running, or batting badminton birds without nets, or playing pick-up games of *futbal* and hockey. My friends were as mad about *futbal* as I about football. They played it on grass, in the courtyard, on snow, and in the dorm corridor. They were true *sportsmeny* and worthy of the athletic suits they so often wore. I was not good enough to play *futbal* regularly, except in the corridor.

I went skating on the big university rink using university skates, which were free but beat-up. I bought a new pair in a downtown store for eleven rubles. The first time I used them it was twenty degrees below zero and I caught a cold.

MGU students go skiing right outside the university gates. They ski crosscountry, and there are no tows on Lenin Hills. Their boots are not much more than heavy shoes, and their modest wood skis are inexpensive. The usual ski outfit is a baggy blue sweat suit with a sweater, and that goes for girls, too.

Once I had the gall to step out on the practice court with the MGU varsity basketball team. They, bless them, seemed to assume that any American must be a wizard at the game. Their best players were good—no Bill Bradleys, but good enough to make an American college team. I was soft and wheezy and not the marksman I had been in junior high school, the best days I ever saw on the court. In thirty minutes of play I managed to sink only two baskets. But I did tell a couple of anecdotes about "Wilt the Stilt" Chamberlain and escaped with a small piece of my pride intact.

The only place I could play the Russians even was in front of the *televizor*—television set—and the only games I could beat them at were baseball and frisbee. The problem with the *televizor* was getting within forty cheering bodies of it. The lounge was so crowded and noisy for big *futbal* and hockey telecasts that the first time I saw the mob I thought it was another Vietnam protest rally. The spirit of the viewers, the way they sat on the edge of their seats, the way they razzed each other, cheered and hissed the players, and mimicked the announcer, all this reminded me of American college men watching the world series or pro football on television. The Russians lacked only commercials to mock, but they found plenty to ignore in the speeches by Party leaders and uplifting newscasts at half time. They argued about which game to watch; and when the *televizor* was out of order on the seventeenth floor, the sports fans trooped down to "nationalize" the set on the sixteenth floor, where more cultured viewers were trying to take in a concert.

A Russian I knew had a *televizor* in his room, a rare luxury at MGU. He was choosy about inviting his guests, but even a small select company had to take up positions on tables, the bed, and the floor of the crowded little room. The lounge was just as cramped. It was hot, even in winter, and spectators were usually limp at the end. The same fellows who had besieged me with questions at the *punkt* merely waved a greeting and then concentrated on the game. Once I was asked to explain American baseball and football, but I didn't have the Russian vocabulary to encompass concepts such as balls and strikes, offensive holding, and, especially, the Statue of Liberty play. Eventually, the sight of the American team floundering pitifully in the World Hockey Championship created a bond of sports sympathy among us. "How can a great country like yours send a lousy hockey team?" Russians asked me before the big Soviet-American match, which we all expected to be a Soviet massacre. I answered that our best players skated in the professional leagues, but that cut no ice; the Russians insisted on being sympathetic. They had all been hoping to see the game between U.S.S.R. and U.S.A., but they were almost relieved when it was not broadcast into Moscow and I was spared the patriotic pain. After the American defeat, a delegation of fans brought me condolences. "Wait till next year," they said.

Then there was baseball on the lawn in front of MGU's main entrance. Another American and I played with Latin Americans from assorted national liberation movements—Cubans, Panamanians, Venezuelans—whose hatred of Yankee imperialism apparently exempted Yankees like Mickey Mantle and Latin bourgeoisie like Juan Marichal. They had their own bats and well-oiled gloves, but they asked me to borrow a new ball from the American Embassy. I promised to get one from the Marines who guard the gate but never did. We used a battered ball, but the Russians who came around to watch and try their hand at the strange game never knew the difference.

Frisbee, the plastic flying saucer that is fashionable on American campuses, was a revelation to the Russians. Another American and I sailed it back and forth across the courtyard one Sunday afternoon, attracting excited students who asked to apprentice themselves to us in the occult art of flipping the thing. Several inexperienced Soviets sailed the disk into *babushkas* crossing the yard and were scolded at length. A youngster whom I recognized as one of the elevator joy riders offered to trade four Lenin *znachki*—pins with Lenin's portrait—for the frisbee. And several passers-by who asked whether I bought the *tarelochka*—little plate—in GUM were startled to hear that I had obtained it in Cambridge, Massachusetts.

After my success in the yard I decided to introduce the frisbee to the sports fans on my floor. The narrowness of the corridor was a handicap but a friend of mine did not duck a sporting challenge. First he decapitated the *kommandantsha's* favorite giant green plant, and then grazed some smokers shooting the breeze at the *punkt*. "One last throw from around the corner," he said, and flipped the frisbee straight into the face of the leader of our floor, who was innocently emerging from his *blok*.

I expected the worst, including an extra turn at *dezhurstvo,* but our leader smiled. "Let's see that thing," he said. "How do you throw it?"

Sometime after that my friend proposed that I sail the frisbee out of an eighteenth-floor window so that he could try to catch it on the street below. I waited at the window until he appeared in view near the main entrance of the university. Then I climbed onto a table to give me a better angle, and while my friend's girl friend held my feet to keep me from following the frisbee, I flung it out the window. Down below, my friend circled, like Willie Mays waiting to make the catch, but the frisbee circled too, headed back toward the building, and just missed breaking a window on the thirteenth floor.

This same daring sportsman induced me to play a part in another of his pranks. He had connected his tape recorder to the *priomniki* belonging to his neighbor and a *blok* of girls by stringing wires across the hall and along the ledge outside the windows. The parties of the second and third parts had requested the link-up to get taped music as well as the usual radio fare, but the system's prank potential was enormous. My friend had taped a twenty-one-gun salute during the last anniversary of the Revolution celebration, and he was thinking of transmitting the deafening din at some apt moment, like the dead of night. He also was prepared to startle his subscribers by broadcasting a "Big Brother is watching you" announcement. As far as I knew he never got up the nerve to do either, but he did offer "a program of unusual interest."

"*Dorogie tovarishchi* (Dear comrades)," my friend announced over the closed circuit. "You are about to hear a first in Soviet Socialist broadcasting. We present a program of bourgeois ballads." It was my job to sing "Clementine," which Russians knew because they sang it in high school English classes, and I managed to sing a stanza or two before the girls realized they were being duped and rushed into the studio. I was pleased to meet the girls, and during the life of the system I made the acquaintance of other Russians who tripped over the wire strung across the hall.

Music and sports introduced me to many Russians, but in other cases the going was slower. There were times I held back, not only with the eager Americaphiles, but also with students evidently delegated to meet me. Two representatives of the MGU Student Council welcomed me to the university and offered to become my friends, but they made me feel as if they were fulfilling some kind of plan. "How interesting it would be to become acquainted with an American," said one with excessive formality. "We could compare courses of study, fashions of dress, and the eating habits of our two peoples."

Just the opposite was the exuberant Armenian graduate student I met in the *dieticheskaia stolovaia.* He clapped his hands together and congratulated himself on his good luck in meeting an American. After dinner he insisted that we go to a movie showing at MGU, and since the house was sold out, he canvassed strangers trading tickets in the lobby. He appeared devastated when he could not raise a single ticket to honor "Armenian-American" friendship, but he promised success another time and invited me to meet his wife the next evening.

He did not keep the appointment. And when I saw him next he looked at me shamefacedly and said nothing. His wife, who was with him, glared at me coldly. She was a Russian. Had she warned him to keep his distance from an American?

I had the feeling that history was repeating itself when I met two gregarious graduate students from Armenia's neighbor Azerbaijan. When they invited me at once to an impromptu party, I accepted and followed them to the *blok* where one of them lived. While our host, who had been working all day at his desk, cleared away a mess of papers, his friend ran down to the store for bread and sausage, vodka and champagne. Then we pulled the table over to the bed, sat down, and had a feast. A pomegranate brought from Baku by the host was the *pièce de résistance*. "The state trading organization doesn't ship enough pomegranates to Moscow to meet the demand," he said. "If we didn't have restrictions, some enterprising middleman could make millions shipping fruit to Moscow."

"Baku is a much friendlier city than Moscow," said the other Azerbaijani. "There is less crime in Baku because people there take care of each other." He recalled reading that thirty-eight New Yorkers had witnessed the murder of Katherine Genovese without coming to her aid or even calling the police. "In Moscow people would have called the police," he said. "But in Baku eight out of ten neighbors would have rushed down to help her."

Azerbaijani hospitality demanded that we eat and drink as

if we hadn't just done that and never would again. When I could absorb no more they begged me to have one more in honor of some Azerbaijani patriot—I must admit I was too full of vodka to remember the name—and to any American hero of my choice. I chose Thomas Jefferson. At the evening's end, when we separated, they invited me to a *futbal* match between the *neftianiki*—Oilers—of Baku and a Moscow team two days later.

The game took place in the evening and the temperature was near zero. I wore virtually everything I owned—long underwear, a wool shirt, a sweater, ski parka and scarf, fur hat, two pairs of socks, and boots. My friends, to my amazement, had on only thin plastic raincoats as outer garments, apparently counting on their enthusiasm and their compatriots to keep them warm. There were only 3,000 fans in Lenin Stadium, which seats more than 100,000, but at least half of them were Azerbaijanis, and they huddled together. Friends of my friends seemed delighted to have me root for Baku. What was amusing and touching was that they were concerned that I, who was most warmly dressed of all, would freeze and endanger Azerbaijani-American relations. I use the phrase Azerbaijani-American instead of Soviet-American advisedly; it was their phrase.

Moscow won. The game was dull. And why not? The boys from Baku, a city on the Caspian where winters are mellow, ran as if congealed. Leaving the stadium we ran along the Moscow River embankment to the subway and shivered all the way home. The university was warm and inviting and I looked forward to warming up on coffee or something stronger with my friends.

But as soon as I entered the university I changed my mind. A familiar figure was leaning against the wall inside the door, a short nondescript man in a brown suit. He followed us through the lobby to the central section. He stopped and watched us when we stopped to talk.

I told my friends I had work to do and could not stop by their place. I thanked them for the tickets—for which they refused to take money—and then headed for my elevator. The man in the brown suit followed, walking about five yards behind me, not saying a word. He didn't follow me upstairs.

9

Me and My Shadows

THE stocky little men in shabby brown suits. They are an indivisible part of my memories of my stay in Moscow. The man I saw when I was saying good-bye to my Azerbaijani friends was familiar. I had seen him before and was to encounter him again. He was one of a tribe whose business obviously was surveillance.

I had expected that sort of thing, as well as other hazards. In past years I had read in the Soviet press of American exchange students charged with anti-Soviet activity, and I knew that several had been asked to leave the country. I had heard rumors of attempts to blackmail Americans lured into compromising situations, and I had read enough spy stories to imagine a few gaudy details of my own.

Watch out for false friends! Protect true Soviet friends! Do not introduce Russians to each other! Warn naïve Russians that their own police may be watching and listening! These were the warnings from Americans who knew or thought they knew. But how do you tell a Russian to beware of his own countrymen? Don't Russians know the facts of their own lives?

The year before I had also been warned—needlessly. I was

never followed, as far as I could tell, and certainly no one sought to ensnare me or, worse luck, seduce me. Living at MGU, I would suspect occasionally, whenever the James Bond mood was upon me, that the walls might be bugged, the phone tapped, and infrared cameras hidden in nooks and crannies. But in the beginning I didn't have time to worry. I was ignored.

Suspicions were miles from my mind when I came down from my room one autumn morning to buy milk in the MGU grocery store. I left the elevator on the second floor landing and turned onto the mezzanine, which overlooks the first floor lobby and entrance. To my right was the short passage which leads to the stairs and past them into the central zone. All students had to walk through this passage to enter and leave the Zone V dormitory area, and usually a woman sat at a check point monitoring traffic. On this particular morning the corridor was crowded with students hurrying to classes.

As soon as I saw the two types leaning against the wall just beyond the checkpoint, I knew. They looked too old to be students, too much like pugilists to be professors, too well-dressed to be handymen; and they were the only persons in the place not rushing somewhere. They never moved, but their heads turned and their eyes followed me as I passed them; and they stared at me when I returned from the store.

Was I imagining things? I thought that I was. An hour later I went downstairs again, as much to test my suspicions as to pick up my mail at the MGU post office. The two were still there and again gazed at me with brazen directness. As I stood in line in the post office, one entered, looked me in the eye for a moment, then left. Could they be secret police? If so, they were blatantly unsecretive.

I tried to suspend judgment until lunchtime. But I was still uneasy when I set out for the *stolovaia.* The two were nowhere in sight when I walked past the checkpoint toward the central zone. Nor was there any sign of them as I stood in line waiting for a table. As I sat down to eat, one entered the dining room, followed in a moment by his buddy, who passed right in front of my table. Each glanced at the posted menu, then at me, and then took up a position leaning against the wall outside the *stolovaia.*

By now I had no doubt. But I wanted to be absolutely sure. I got up and strolled through the lobby, stopping at newsstands to look at magazines. One of my uninvited companions stopped three feet away from me. I examined an exhibit of East German photos. My unwanted pal stood near me and scrutinized it, too. I went out into the courtyard. They stood in the doorway watching. I entered Zone V again and nearly bumped into one of them in the revolving door.

Now I was sure. The next question was, Why were they following me and why so openly at that? Since they surely could keep track of me less obviously, their tactics must have some other purpose. To intimidate me? To frighten off my Soviet friends? Would they always be waiting downstairs? Would they follow me away from the university and all around town? Would they follow other American students as well? Whatever the purpose and whatever its future pattern, the tailing had an immediate effect. I had a date with a Russian girl who was to show me around the botanical gardens of the university. But I could just see the four of us tiptoeing through the tulips. I didn't know how to get in touch with her to beg off. So I simply didn't show up. Later, when Soviet friends didn't keep appointments with me, I wondered if they had similar reasons.

For the next two weeks I saw the two men often, as well as another ten who seemed to do the same work on different shifts. I wasn't followed all the time, and as far as I knew I was never tailed upstairs to my room. But more often than not I had company, not of my own choosing, at a meal a day at the university. My buddies strolled to the bus stops and taxi stand a step behind me, but I didn't notice anyone following me downtown. Sometimes they picked me up at the elevators. Other times I saw the woman at the checkpoint run to the phone when I passed, and then one of the men took up my trail in the central zone. Finally there were times when I saw no men, no woman at the checkpoint, no sign at all, until I was seated in the *stolovaia*. Then, as if by magic, a "chum" would appear and find a seat nearby.

After two weeks the tailing stopped, and for the next three months the brown-suited men didn't bother me at all. Now and then I caught sight of one, and I felt, for a weird moment, that I ought to hail him as an old acquaintance. But when he saw me he ducked out of sight. I guessed they formed a contingent based at MGU, but apparently I was no longer in their Plan.

Early in January as I was waiting for the elevator one of the men I had first seen in the fall walked up to within five feet of my nose and stared, signaling the resumption of hostilities. But in the new phase, which lasted until I left the Soviet Union, the pattern was altered. Inside the university the shadowing covered the same ground—downstairs corridors, *stolovaias,* bus stops, and the taxi stand, but it was sporadic. And for the first time I began to be followed downtown. As far as I know that happened only a few times. It was most obvious when I took a taxi. As I walked out to the taxi stand in front of the main entrance, one of the regulars would appear, wait nearby while I gave instructions to my driver, and then signal a car waiting a few yards away, in which sat another crew. Obviously the outside men were taking over. It was these characters who trailed me downtown, on the metro, to the theater, into restaurants, and even into Lenin Library, where I couldn't believe the white-haired man reading documents at the next table was one of them until he followed me downstairs and pointed me out to another man, who followed me the rest of the day.

My encounters with my shadows had their ironic and ludicrous aspects. In my early days at MGU, when I had no friends to join up front on the *stolovaia* line, they would take places behind me at the rear. What blessing it would have been if they had taken places up front! In that case I might have been tempted to join them.

Sometimes the chase reminded me of the Keystone cops. One morning I was walking down a long narrow corridor to the laundry room in the basement with one of them right behind. I turned a corner, discovered that the room was closed, started back and bumped right into him. *"Izvinite,"* I said. Excuse me. But he never replied, and I strode off in the opposite direction with him at my heels.

Another time I finished eating just as they were sitting down to eat in the *stolovaia.* I dumped my empty dishes on the counter and turned to go. They jumped up and tried to dump bowls full of borsch and plates of *kapusta* (cabbage). But in his hurry to pick up my trail, one man splattered crimson borsch on his brown suit.

Since my shadows' strategy was to make me notice them, I tried to ignore them. I chose not to play obvious games with them. I didn't duck behind phone booths trying to lose them. I didn't snap their pictures pretending to take national monuments. I resisted the temptation to fling a fast ball at them as they stood nonchalantly watching me play baseball in front of MGU. But I couldn't resist the temptation to try to tweak their noses without seeming to.

One rainy day I was standing under the shelter of an awning, and one of them was standing right next to me, when it occurred to me that I had an umbrella and he didn't. I waited for a particularly drenching downpour and marched out into it. He dutifully followed and took the soaking consequences. Another time a trio—two men and a woman—walked behind me from the metro to the university on a hot and muggy day. I steadily increased the pace and did the distance like an Olympic marathon walker. My followers were wet with perspiration and breathing hard when they arrived.

However comical the chase was at times, it was also unnerving. I couldn't very well strike up acquaintances with strangers in the *stolovaia* with two flatfoots sitting at the next table. I hesitated to attend another Vietnam protest rally. I didn't dare look up relatives of a Russian I knew in New York. I couldn't be too friendly with my Soviet friends.

Or could I? It was not illegal. Why be so cautious? Perhaps the police were interested only in me and would not bother my Russian friends. Perhaps my friends would laugh the whole thing off if I told them.

I didn't tell any Russians about the tailing for a long time. It wasn't my responsibility to point it out if they didn't see it, nor was it sensible to frighten them if they weren't frightened. I tried to act normally, as if I didn't hear the footsteps or see the shadows. But I couldn't act normally, especially on Easter Eve.

I had taken a *studentka* to a concert at the Moscow Conservatory and we were leaving to meet her friends when I noticed two men watching us across the street. They walked behind us to the trolley stop; one leaped on behind us just before the doors closed, and the other raced to a waiting car.

When we arrived at our friends' apartment house I was invited upstairs. But I couldn't help noticing the familiar car a few yards away at the curb. I said I would wait downstairs, but my friends, who hadn't noticed the men or the car, looked at me as if I were crazy. "But you're invited," they said. "Don't be shy. Come on." I thought of pleading a headache and going home. Reluctantly I went upstairs.

We left the apartment, where we had had tea, and walked to a church. Looking back I saw the two men walking behind us, and behind them the crawling car. We had hoped to stand through the service, but the church was filled to capacity and outside a phalanx of police was turning away people who kept pressing toward the doors. The street around the church was crowded, too, and residents hung out of apartment house windows watching worshipers who couldn't get in—mostly old women who held lighted candles and waited patiently for midnight, when the procession would emerge, circle the church, and reenter it. Many who were obviously curiosity seekers stood quietly, too, but not the rowdy zoot-suited teen-agers who ran through the crowd taunting worshipers and scuffling with police, who tried from time to time to corral the most obnoxious hecklers. Several old women attempted to admonish the youngsters, telling them to have respect for their elders and let them pray in peace, but that only made the toughs laugh more insolently. My friends were not believers, but they took no part in the heckling and appeared to be embarrassed by it. Perhaps they sought to share on this holy night the feeling of the worshipers, to understand the force which brought these old women, many of them bent and feeble, to stand for hours in the cold, clutching their candles, crossing themselves, waiting for the hour when "*Khristos voskres.*" My friends bought candles, too, and after straining for a glimpse of the altar through a window, they proposed that we make a last try to sneak past the uniformed policemen into the church. But my shadows were at my shoulder, apparently trying not to lose me in the crush. I said I would wait outside. I said that an American in Moscow could not afford to run afoul of the law. My friends laughed and teased me about being timid, when one the shadows pushed by me and tapped my date on the arm. "Do you have the time?" he asked, looking right at me, and his partners, who were right behind him, grinned. I froze, but the girl, who suspected nothing, told him the time.

We never did try to enter the church, and after the midnight procession we walked slowly back to the Russians' apartment. By the time we reached the house it was very late. Buses and subways were no longer running, and it would be difficult to find a taxi. My friends suggested that I sleep over at their place, but looking across the street I saw the shadowy figures standing in the doorway beside their car. I said I couldn't stay, thanked them anyway, and set out to look for a cab.

Being tailed was disturbing. But even worse was to imagine things. Once I saw a figure standing on the roof staring in the direction of my room through field glasses. Was he spying on me? A beautiful girl sat down at my table in a downtown restaurant and opened a copy of the United States Information Agency magazine, *Amerika.* Was this an obvious come-on? "I'm an American," I said, testing her. "How do you like our magazine?" She was startled and looked almost frightened. She mumbled something unintelligible, hurriedly finished her meal, and left. Some come-on! The right word was brush-off.

I knew a West European who had been studying at MGU for five years under auspices that were never quite clear to me. He had embarrassed me several times by making loud anti-Soviet remarks in the *stolovaia,* but I dismissed that as bad manners. Then he invited me to a rally protesting the trial of Sinyavsky and Daniel. I was tempted to go but declined. The next day I heard that police had arrested the demonstrators and taken the names of bystanders. Had the invitation been a trap?

One evening, quite late, a lovely sloe-eyed young woman in a low-cut formfitting dress came to my room to propose that I help her with her English. I had been helping a few students on my floor, but this girl said she was not an MGU *studentka,* and she was very vague about how she had managed to get into the university without a *propusk.* She said she had looked on the list of residents for names that sounded American. It is true that Russian girls tend to be natural and informal—but not that bold. I suggested that she come back in the morning. She returned the next evening, again quite late, wearing the same come-hither costume. Again I told her I was busy and suggested that she phone before dropping in again. A week later she buzzed my room from the *punkt* and when I came out to see who was calling, I found her surrounded by the usual loungers and smokers at the *punkt.* I had heard in the meantime that she had approached several other Americans with the same linguistic proposition. Was she merely an imaginative, enterprising girl out to improve her English and meet some Americans? Or had she been assigned to tempt us? The boys at the *punkt* listened attentively while she invited herself to my room, I said I was eating, she said she would wait while I ate, and I said sorry, *do svidaniia*—good-bye.

"Do svidaniia?" exclaimed one of the boys. "Are you crazy or something? Why turn down a *devka* (babe) like that?"

Why indeed? It's tough to be suspicious in Moscow, but it could be tougher not to.

Another evening an attractive physics *studentka* knocked at my door seeking help in translating a scholarly paper which she was to deliver to an International Physics Congress. She too was a complete stranger, and as I glanced through the complicated mathematical formulas, I thought of Yale Professor Frederick Barghoorn, who was arrested in Moscow holding a planted document in his hand. Was the material harmless? Was the girl on the level? I was sick and tired of being suspicious. I decided to help her. She sat down next to me at my desk, and we had done half a page when there was another knock at the door.

I had never seen the slight, balding young man who now entered my room and asked for Pavel Ivanovitch Somethingorotherskii.

"He doesn't live here," I said.

"But he must live here," he replied.

"But he doesn't," I said again.

He took out a cigarette, lit it, dragged deeply, and sat down on the bed.

"I know who I want," he said, now speaking in poor English. "I want you."

Was this at last the real thing? I wondered, feeling none of Raskolnikov's relief, because I had committed no crime and hence deserved no punishment.

"What do you want?" I asked, trying not to reveal what I was thinking.

"I want your help in studying English."

"But you asked for a Russian when you knocked," I said.

He smiled a sickly Peter Lorre smile, glanced at the girl who was sitting calmly at my desk, and looked at me again.

"I think you can help me," he said.

"I'm afraid I have no time," I said, beginning to get angry.

"You have time. I'm sure you have time," he said.

Suddenly it occurred to me that his poor English might be giving the conversation its sinister tone, that he might be speaking simply and repeating himself because he knew no other words, that he might be smiling because he was embarrassed. I switched to Russian and said again I was sorry, but I had no time to help him. But he insisted I had time. Finally I walked to within an inch of his chin, and told him I had not invited him, that he was bothering me, and that he could get out. He got to his feet slowly, bowed once to the girl, smiled once more at me, and left without a word.

Was this intimidation, too? Or was it a nasty little coincidence? I didn't know. I finished helping the girl with the translation.

The incident did resolve one question in my mind. I decided to tell my Soviet friends about what had been happening to me. If these strangers were going to such lengths to upset me, it was time to take counsel with my Russian friends.

One fellow blanched when I told him of my adventures and avoided me from that moment on. Another chap rubbed his hands gleefully and rushed off to tell all his friends about what was going on right there in MGU. I showed a Russian friend the joker on the roof who looked at me through field glasses. My friend amazed me by running to the window and shouting across the courtyard, "Who the hell are you? Stop spying on people!" My friend even offered to climb to the roof if I would keep the man occupied.

Some Russians told me to relax and forget it. They said tailing was inevitable in the cold war, that secret policemen had to do something for their pay, and that the FBI probably follows Soviet exchange students in the U.S.A.

"Don't worry about agents," said one Russian. "Everybody's got them."

"Let's not be naïve," another student said. "The FBI and the KGB—the Soviet Committee on State Security—may be archenemies, but they have more in common with each other than either one has with the liberals of its own society. They each see enemies in every corner; they're trained and paid to do that."

A *Pravda* correspondent who had spent seven years in America told a lounge full of MGU students about his adventures with the FBI. According to his story, they included the following: When he tried to interview strikers on a New York picket line, an agent openly took notes of the conversation scaring away the strikers. When he traveled around the country by car, a car full of agents followed right behind. When he lingered too long over lunch at the side of the road, the FBI car pulled up alongside and the agents said they were ready to move on. When the correspondent refused to move on and went for a stroll instead, he found his tires slashed when he returned. The agents spent so much time in his house that he took to leaving beer in the refrigerator for them.

The Soviet students roared with laughter at the correspondent's tale, and I laughed too, but not quite comfortably. Suppose the journalist was telling the truth? Aren't American journalists in Moscow harassed by Soviet agents? Even as I was silently framing the question, the speaker provided the answer.

"You can bet," he said, "that every time word gets back here that a Soviet correspondent has been bedeviled in the U.S.A., something similar happens to an American journalist in Moscow."

I cannot be certain, but I gathered that I was followed more than any other American student, some of whom told me that they were not disturbed at all. Was this because my research topic was contemporary and might cause me to pry into closed crannies of Moscow society? Were historians studying eighteenth-century diplomacy in the archives considered less of a threat? Was I suspect because my knowledge of Russian enabled me to roam more widely than some of the others? Or was my tour as interpreter for the Soviet Basketball Team responsible? After all, Americans touring the Soviet Union are constantly fearful that their guides are really spying on them. Wouldn't it be natural for Soviet travelers in America to have similar suspicions of their American interpreters and guides?

I kept recalling the trip with the basketball team at moments of greatest strain, when it seemed as if squadrons of secret police were detailed to observe and follow me. Could any of it have been innocent, like the time in Las Vegas when a sheriff, a police chief, and a host of deputies and troopers wearing Sam Brown belts and low-slung six-shooters guarded the players at the hotel, at the game, and at the nightspot afterwards? Did their presence bother the Russians? When the lawmen joined the visitors at their table and asked proudly whether they had ever seen babes like that, did that take the edge off the Russians' fun? By the time we left Las

Vegas the deputies and the Soviet players were trading souvenirs, bullets and pins of the Nevada State Law Officers' Association in return for *znachki* with Lenin's portrait.

As for me and my shadows, I tried to see them in perspective. After all, it could have been worse. They might have tailed me on New Year's Eve, or to the student wedding, but they didn't. Or did they?

10

New Year's Eve

BECAUSE it is a religious holiday, Christmas is not officially celebrated in the Soviet Union. But the New Year is, and miraculously enough toward the end of December there began at MGU a bustle and preparation that made it seem as if Christmas were indeed approaching.

Russians ran out to purchase gifts to be exchanged at New Year's, and they bought, addressed, and mailed their New Year's cards. They decked the halls, not with holly, but with gaily colored New Year's bulbs and banners. Two *studentki* on my floor unveiled a New Year's tree which they themselves had cut down in the woods on Lenin Hills and trimmed with silver tinsel. And the MGU *stolovaias* laid out a pre-New Year's bazaar including holiday treats from other parts of the Soviet Union and East Europe, items like fresh tangerines and special wines, which were so rare that they almost never appeared in MGU stores.

In the midst of the preparations, some Russians found time to console an American who was far from home and Christmas. The representatives of the Student Council, who had greeted me so stiffly in the fall, returned to make a formal presentation of a Christmas card printed in English. Doing his duty with complete solemnity, the spokesman wished me a "very Merry Christmas" and allowed, with a sympathetic sigh, that I must be pining for Christmas at home. I responded with equal seriousness, thanking them gravely and admitting to a certain nostalgia. Then, to assuage their concern, I added that I wouldn't miss the excessively commercialized aspects of Christmas in America.

A more sophisticated Russian, who understood the similarities between Christmas in New York and New Year's in Moscow, tried to play it straight. "All these decorations and banners and bulbs must seem so new and strange to you," he said with the air of a guide showing a new world to a tourist. "All these pagan rituals in an atheistic state must shock someone who's accustomed to the simple devotions of Christmas." In spite of himself, his eyes were dancing with laughter.

Students who had money for travel and didn't live thousands of miles away in Vladivostok went home for the holiday. Other hardy souls went off on low-cost trade union vacations to sports camps, where, as one vacationer recalled afterwards, "We lived ten to a room, washed up in the morning in the snow, didn't read a newspaper, skated on the lake, skied in the woods, danced to someone's tape recorder, and played cards by lantern after they put out the lights at 11:30."

But travel funds were limited and so were the available places in sports camps, and many of my Russian colleagues remained at MGU on New Year's Eve.

I dropped by the Gala New Year's Eve Ball on my way to a party and found the first two floors of the central zone filled with revels and revelers. Under the balloons and the streamers five—count 'em—five combos were playing. Three groups were belting out the big beat for twisting and frugging dancers and making up in noise for what they lacked in subtlety. A fourth played for Russian folk dancing, and here the musicians were truly in their element. And a fifth thumped out a rhythmic accompaniment for community folk singing led by a big plump round-faced woman in an old-fashioned orange evening gown who perspired freely as she sang and held aloft large cards carrying the verses of the songs. In the university's 1,500-seat *Aktovyi Zal*—Assembly Hall—a stage show "featuring top variety artists" was holding forth, and another show was going on in the MGU theater. Two films were showing in two other auditoriums. The *dieticheskaia* and *professorskaia stolovaias* were decked out with awnings and checkered tablecloths, and all doors were open so that students could move freely among all the attractions.

It was several hours before midnight. I stood in the lobby of Zone V waiting to meet a girl and watching young Russians on their way to the ball. They ran coatless through the swirling snow across the freezing courtyard, and when they entered the lobby they shook off the flakes and scampered up the stairs toward the central zone. I couldn't help but notice that their finery was not so fine, that while some girls wore chic gowns and smart seamless stockings, others looked dowdy in shapeless dresses and cotton stockings. A few boys wore stylish continental suits, obviously saved for special occasions, but others had on the same shiny outfits they wore to classes. I saw no mod costumes, no mini-skirts or pants suits, and no Beatle haircuts. By Western standards, their dress was conservative, if not stodgy. And yet their clothes were the only stodgy thing about them. Their freshly scrubbed faces were shining from the cold, and with their youthful enthusiasm they reminded me of lively young Americans at a college dance. Once they began twisting and frugging, East looked as if it had become part of the West.

Two young Russians were waiting for their dates in the lobby, too, when a short round old woman walked wearily by, a cleaning lady on her way home, the only traffic moving out into the cold. She looked like a tired little tea cozy in her long brown overcoat with scarves wrapped snuggly about her neck and ears.

"S novym godom (Happy New Year) , *babushka,"* said one of the boys.

"S novym godom to you, young man," clucked the *babushka,* smiling kindly through her scarves. "May you have a good life, *mal'chiki.* And may you find a wonderful pure love."

"Why a pure love?" asked one of the *mal'chiki* playfully.

"May you live happily and love purely," she cooed again and looked at all three of us benevolently. "The younger generation is sometimes hard to understand. Why, I saw a film in which a boy and girl were kissing, kissing, kissing; and then she slapped his face. *Eto zhe nenormal'no* (that's just not normal) ."

"Wasn't that an outrageous thing for that girl to do!" exclaimed the boy.

"In my day," continued the old woman, who had a faraway look in her eye and had not noticed the interruption, "why, in my day we were kissed; we were kissed, too. But we didn't slap their faces."

"But *babushka,"* put in the student, "Russian girls have deteriorated since the Revolution."

"And what about Russian boys?" she asked. "Haven't they deteriorated, too?"

"Oh, no. We're still as good as ever," he replied.

The old woman chuckled deep in her throat and shook her head. Then she wrapped the scarves even more warmly about her head and walked slowly toward the door where she bumped into the French girl who was coming to meet me.

"Now here's a lovely Russian girl," said the old woman, "and just as nice as any before 1917."

"Yes, indeed," the boys agreed.

"S novym godom, mal'chiki," said the old woman. *"Do svidaniia."*

The party I was headed for was one of many taking place upstairs in the rooms of students who preferred private gatherings to the mass celebration downstairs. I had been invited by Russians I knew only casually, and I wasn't sure what kind of reception to expect. Furthermore, I had taken it upon myself to invite the French girl, also an exchange student at MGU, at the last minute. I wasn't sure if that would be considered a breach of etiquette, and I wondered whether we would fit in.

I needn't have worried. The guests, who filled both rooms of a *blok,* appeared delighted to have us. They wished us *"s novym godom"* and led us up to the table to take our pick of the food and drink: vodka, wine, and champagne, potato salad and meat salad, sardines and sprats, apples and oranges, cheese and pickles, sausage and bread. I realized that only contributions from everyone could have paid for the spread, but I didn't know how to offer tactfully to pay my share. I hesitantly mumbled something about helping out. I was turned down.

Chairs had been moved into the hall to make room for extra tables, but the room was still jammed. Three men had to stand on the window sill; and two rows of guests, glasses in hand, sat and stood on the bed, looking like a class of wine tasters posing for a graduation picture.

At 11:35 a student standing on the window sill made a brief speech, offering a specially cordial welcome to the *frantsuzhenka* and the *amerikanets.*

At 11:40 I was asked to make a speech, and fortunately I was prepared.

"I would like to present one of the finest fruits of American culture and industry," I declared in my best imitation of a side show barker's voice, then handed out thirty pieces of Double Bubble bubble gum, one to a customer.

"Hurrah for American consumer goods," shouted a Russian delightedly.

"And now," I continued, "I will demonstrate the extraordinary powers of this little pink miracle." But though I struggled mightily, I could not produce a bubble.

The guests groaned, but no one else could pop one either. In fact I was just about to shift their attention to the comic strips that come with the gum, when suddenly the *frantsuzhenka* popped a perfectly spherical, transparently pink doozie.

"In honor of de Gaulle!" shouted a Russian.

"A marriage of French technology to American pure science and basic research," yelled another.

At 11:50 a critical question was posed by the man on the window sill: When should we drink the champagne, at the first stroke of midnight, or the sixth or the twelfth? And when should the kissing take place? A vote was taken. It was decided to cheer at the first chime, drink at the sixth, and kiss at the twelfth.

At 11:55 the announcer on the radio, who was intoning the Communist Party's official New Year's greeting, blasted American imperialism one last time in 1965. I bowed my head in a mockery of guilt and shame.

"Ignore the radio," said a Russian contemptuously as he patted me on the shoulder.

"It's just propaganda," added another scornfully.

"Forget it. It's just *erunda* (nonsense) ," said a third.

The first chime of the New Year sounded on the radio. We cheered. At the sixth stroke, we downed the champagne. With the twelfth stroke, as the radio struck up the national anthem, kisses flew in all directions and neither the *frantsuzhenka* nor I was left out.

11

The Wedding Party

SHORTLY after the New Year I was invited to become a member of a Soviet *svad'ba* (wedding). Katia, a Russian girl whom I dated occasionally, asked me to accompany her. I knew the couple casually, but she was a close friend of the bride and bridegroom.

Student weddings are not uncommon at MGU. After the ceremony the newlyweds go on with their studies and continue to receive their stipends. The bride moves into the bridegroom's *blok* where, as you remember, they share only one room.

At MGU married couples even manage to start raising families in one room. But my impression was that the logistics of that kind of upbringing are not easy. I knew husbands and wives who took turns going off to a library or the lounge to study, while the other remained behind to watch the baby. There was one chap who set up his desk in the vestibule of his *blok*—and if that wasn't cramped, I don't know what is. In fact on occasion this fellow, probably overcome by claustrophobia or nearly asphyxiated by the smoke of his own cigarettes, would take refuge in the hall, where he would read standing under a bare bulb. Some passers-by respected his absorption in his work. But others stopped to chat; and sometimes if he wanted to continue his reading the harried scholar would have to retreat to his vestibule. Other couples with children, annoyed by loud chattering in the hall, would post signs on their doors: *"Tishe—rebionok spit!* (Quiet—A child is sleeping)."

As happens in other societies, marriages break up at MGU and students seek divorces. A divorce is simpler to obtain in the Soviet Union than in nearly all American states, since the law allows incompatibility as sufficient grounds. But divorce registration fees range from fifty to two hundred rubles, which is expensive for students on stipends, and there are other complications for residents of the MGU dormitory. One of the divorced parties must find another room. A divorcee who wants to keep her child with her needs assistance. If the baby is old enough, it can be left at a crèche for a few hours a day. But in the evening there is no such thing as paid baby-sitting at MGU, and one divorced mother I knew counted on her neighbors to keep an ear tuned for the infant.

As to the couples who chose to share a room without benefit of marriage, there was no legal sanction, I'm sure, for this kind of arrangement. Indeed, the authorities, I think, frowned upon it. But to my knowledge such couples lived together for weeks and months at a time without being disturbed. Some ended up by getting married, and others drifted apart.

Marriage ceremonies could be a formality. I heard of several couples who tied the knot on the spur of the moment by registering at ZAGS (Civil Registrar's Office) and then returned to the dorm to toast the union with a few friends. But the couple to whose wedding I was invited wanted their *svad'ba* to be a memorable occasion. It was to take place in a municipal *Dvorets Brakosochetaniia*—Wedding Palace—which the authorities established some years ago when it became clear that marriages contracted at ZAGS left many

Russians with a sense of loss, a feeling that they were being cheated of the solemnity and joy of the occasion. Relatives were coming from out of town, and a dinner party was planned after the ceremony.

The *den' svad'by*—day of the wedding—was full of surprises for me. I had expected to see the bride in an ordinary dress, but she wore a white bridal gown and veil. (The bridegroom had on a dark suit.) I had assumed that we would take the subway to the *Dvorets,* but in keeping with the spirit of the day, a friend of the couple had ordered a caravan of taxis to transport the entire company from MGU. However, getting to the *Dvorets* on time wasn't so easy, I learned, when all the cabs but mine filled and sped away. Waiting with me in mine was the bride's aunt, who refused to leave without her son, who was unaccountably late, and at the same time fretted even more than I for fear that she would miss the ceremony. Finally her son arrived and scrambled into the cab.

"Is your mood spoiled?" his mother asked him irritably.

"No," he replied.

"Well, mine is, and it's your fault," she grumbled.

It would be more sensible to move on, I thought, than to sit still for recriminations. But even our *voditel'* (taxi driver) , a sour young man who had been surveying the scene morosely, insisted on adding his mite to the discussion. If Americans think that their taxi drivers become too talkative with passengers, they ought to meet a few *voditeli.*

"You've got to be more organized—especially at times like this," said our *voditel'*. Then he slammed his car into gear and took off as if trained in New York traffic. To my complete surprise, he got us to the *Dvorets* ahead of schedule.

The *Dvorets* looked quite ordinary from the outside, a drab two-story building set back in a courtyard. But the scene inside was alive with color. Smiling people attached to a number of wedding parties were milling about the brightly painted corridors. Some guests were waiting to deposit their winter coats in the *garderobe,* and others were waiting to get their coats back. Escorts were busy buying corsages which, in the best Western tradition of uniting commerce and emotion, were selling at the scandalously high price of two rubles fifty kopecks each. Many people were simply trying to locate their friends in the crowd.

I lost my friends immediately, but then found them again in waiting rooms reserved for the bride and her entourage and the bridegroom and his companions. The bridegroom for a wedding ahead of our own was moving out as I entered the waiting room, and I could see the bridegroom for the wedding after us heading down the hall; he would have to wait in the corridor until we left. Our bridegroom was getting a last minute pep talk from his friends, though it was obvious from his eager, expectant face that he didn't need it.

The functionary who supervised the movement of wedding parties according to the established timetable poked her head into the waiting room and invited us into the hall where there occurred a little ceremony of uniting us formally with the ladies of our party, who were coming out of their waiting room. The supervisor asked us to form two lines—men in one and women in the other. Then, at the sound of Mendelssohn's Wedding March blaring from the loudspeaker, we marched at a stately pace down the narrow corridor, brushed by men and women heading for their turns in the waiting room, entered a much larger high-ceilinged room with long red drapes and ornate woodwork, and stopped. We found ourselves facing a long table. The couple stood a few feet in front of the table. The women in our party formed a line to the right of them and the men another to the left.

Behind the table sat three women dressed in black. In an alcove to the side, under a large portrait of Lenin, stood a group of about twenty young people. I couldn't figure out who they were or whether they had any connection with us, although it was clear from their demeanor that they were somehow involved.

"We are gathered here today. . . ." The middle woman behind the table had begun to speak. Obviously she was the chairman, the occasion's ranking official. She delivered a little homily on the virtues of marriage, pausing to hymn the joys of love and enduring devotion.

One of the women at her side—she had the high cheekbones of a Kazakh—stood up and came around the table. She held a ring in her hand and she presented it to the bridegroom without comment. She returned to her seat. The lucky man placed the ring on the fourth finger of the bride's right hand. The couple and the *svideteli*—two men and women in our party—were asked to sign the marriage book. The marriage was sealed. The couple embraced while the rest of us smiled.

Then, to my amazement, the speeches began. The third woman behind the table rose solemnly and walked forward stiffly. As a deputy to Moscow's City Council, she wished to congratulate the newlyweds in the name of the city of Moscow, its government and people. Turning to the group in the alcove, she introduced them as a *delegatsia* from the Higher School of the Komsomol. They were strangers not only to me but to the Russians in our party as well. A young man in the *delegatsia* stepped forward and took a position in front of the table about five feet from the newlyweds. He planted his feet firmly, crossed his arms on his chest and took a deep breath.

"We have come here today to share your great and boundless joy," he declared in tones that were both sugary and pompous.

As he continued with his effusively sentimental oration, I felt a strange sense of déjà vu. He reminded me of a gallery of familiar American types. He was the glib high school kid with aggressive political instincts who ran for every Student Council office. He was the college backslapper who served on every class committee. He was the pumper of hands, the lifelong Boy Scout, the rah-rah raiser of funds. He was the maudlin old grad at the big game. He was full of enthusiasm, emotional and maybe even sincere. *"Vy takie schastlivye liudi, vy takie radostnye liudi, chto . . .* (You are such happy people, you are such joyous people, that I cannot find the words to express the emotion that fills our hearts at the sight of you) ."

I noticed that others in the wedding group were shifting their feet restlessly, and quite a few of them looked relieved when the oration mercifully ended. Next the middle woman in black pushed a button under the table which, I supposed, was the signal for the next wedding party. Then, while the young orator returned to the Komsomol *delegatsia* in the alcove, presumably to be ready to pronounce his sanctimonious benediction on the next defenseless pair, we were escorted out of the room and into another chamber. Here on a table stood bottles of champagne. I wondered how we could possibly have our dinner in this room, with the next company only a few minutes behind us. We didn't. Waitresses were at the ready. They filled our glasses quickly. We drained them to a hasty toast, then filed out to get our coats.

The post-wedding party was to be held in a downtown restaurant, and on the way there the girls in my cab rehearsed the toasts they would make. "How's this for a toast?" asked one of them. "You are such happy people, you are such joyous people, that I cannot find the words to express the emotion which fills our hearts." It was a very good imitation of the Komsomol orator, and the girls went into gales of giggles that lasted the rest of the way to the restaurant.

At the restaurant we had a private room which friends of the couple had decorated with colored streamers. There was a bulletin board on which were mounted photographs showing the bride and bridegroom in cradles, in kindergarten, in high school, in a physics laboratory, and on vacation in the country. Someone had brought a tape recorder from which emerged the beat of Western rock-and-roll drowning out the squarer music of the restaurant's live band.

The toasts began as soon as we were seated. The father of the bride offered a gallant one, but the father of the bridegroom was overcome with emotion and flubbed his.

"Gor'ko. Gor'ko (Bitter. Bitter)," yelled the assembled company in unison until the newlyweds had sweetened the drinks for all by kissing each other.

"Gor'ko," they cried again, demanding that the parents embrace, too, and then again *"gor'ko"* for the *svideteli.* I was just thinking how picturesque the old custom was when someone poked me in the ribs. *"Gor'ko,"* they were calling, and they didn't stop until I bussed the girl sitting next to me.

I had an honored place at the table and I was the fifth guest called upon to make a toast and a short speech. "I have come 8,000 miles just to be here tonight," I began with mock seriousness, "and if you don't understand my toast, it's because I'm speaking in a foreign language and drinking a foreign drink, something called vodka, I think. Our social systems may differ, but at a time like this a man remains a man. And so I drink to mankind and marriage."

I had started out my speech meaning to be playful, but under the influence of the vodka and the general feeling of well-being I had been carried away; and my toast had turned corny and sentimental. I wondered how they would react, and I was relieved to see there was no misunderstanding. They laughed at the beginning of the speech and applauded at the end. I suspect that in the manner of so many good-hearted Russians they were responding with ever fresh wonder to the fact that an American was sharing their occasion, wishing them well and managing to do it in Russian.

We ate, stuffing ourselves on the salads, fish, and meat that cheerful waitresses brought before us. We danced. And then we returned to our seats—believe it or not—for more food. I had been warned that one young man in the company was fervently anti-American and wanted to take me on in debate. Suddenly he was sitting next to me. I feared a scene. But my self-appointed antagonist had long since lost whatever eloquence was his in wine, and the best argument he could muster was a barely intelligible gurgle about Five-Year Plans.

After singing some Russian folk songs, they called on me for "The Saints Go Marching In," and joining hands in a circle every one sang the chorus. They also knew "I've Been Working on the Railroad" and when they didn't know the words to any more American songs, they urged me to sing alone.

Midway in the evening some stylishly dressed young people entered our dining room and introduced themselves as Polish students. They congratulated the young bride and bridgroom and stayed to dance to the rock-and-roll music on our tape recorder. The Poles looked so modish, they held their chins so high in the air and dropped so many names of Western artists and entertainers that the Russians seemed subdued in comparison. Although I was, theoretically, the most Western man in the room, I felt closer to my Russian friends than to the affected Poles.

The evening ended early because the newlyweds had to be at the lab the next morning. Just before I left, the bridegroom's father introduced me to his daughter, a girl of about thirteen who looked like a ballerina.

"She studies English in school," he said, "and would like to speak English with you."

The little girl curtsied charmingly, but despite her father's encouragement all she could do was blush.

With some Russian friends, I returned to the dorm by subway. The happy couple, I learned later, took up their married life in their one room. And there they lived, happily ever after—until the bride was assigned to a lab outside Moscow for an extended tour of duty.

12

What to Play and What to Sing?

MEMBERS of an MGU theater group were doing an American play, and knowing that a number of Americans were living at MGU, they decided to seek advice. They heard that I had done some college dramatics and came to me for help.

The group, called the International Student Theater because it invited foreign students to participate in its productions, was one of two student troupes at MGU. It was based in the *Dom Kul'tury* on Lenin Hills; the other was at the downtown campus. Actors in the group—students, former students, and others—studied the craft under the guidance of professionals while preparing the group's productions. New recruits worked their way up to become what were termed, in the style of the Politburo, "candidate members" and "full members." Whatever status they achieved was decided by a vote of the *kollektiv*.

The American play was an adaptation of a screenplay by Nathan E. Douglas and Harold Jacob Smith for Stanley Kramer's *The Defiant Ones,* a movie that had recently been showing at MGU and around Moscow. This is the story of two convicts, Negro and white, who escape from a Southern chain gang, still chained together. The Russians renamed it *Skovannye tsepiu* (*Bound by a Chain*). An African student, from the Cameroons, was playing the Sidney Poitier role, and a Russian was acting the convict portrayed in the film by Tony Curtis. The sheriff, state police captain, deputies, and troopers who pursue the convicts, and the mob of whites who try to lynch them, were Russians and two Czechs.

I was invited to a rehearsal where a spokesman explained that they wanted me to sit in on preparations to advise them on costumes and local color and to tell them, in all frankness, if the production rang true and if not how it distorted American life.

What I saw at the first rehearsal reminded me of Harvard student productions. These players were more experienced than actors in Winthrop House musical comedies, but they were equally stage-struck, and their enthusiasm and high spirits were equally infectious. Those on stage continually disrupted the rehearsal by flubbing their lines and then laughing at the mistakes. Their pals in the wings made matters worse by egging them on until the director blew his top. One absent actor—he was supposed to play the trainer of dogs used in pursuit of the convicts—was apparently a chronic truant, and the group began to consider whether or not to banish him from the studio. But the debate on this question quickly turned into a good-humored discussion of one of the absentee's favorite bits, an apparently hilarious imitation of the pack of baying bloodhounds he was supposed to direct in the play. His peers mellowed rapidly as they recalled how his howling had cracked up the group at past rehearsals and imagined how he would have done so again had he bothered to show up at this one. In the end, after several other members had imitated the patented imitation, it was decided that a man should have a chance to speak (or bark, someone said) in his own defense before he was banished. The matter was tabled.

Although I felt at home in this atmosphere, I hesitated to agree to their proposal. I couldn't help suspecting that they were doing the play to attack a shabby side of American life. Not that I ducked the problem of racial discrimination while in the U.S.S.R.; I didn't shrink from discussing it because I was glad to make the point that Americans are aware of the problem and are trying to solve it. But if this play was going to be converted into an attack on the United States, I wanted no part of it.

But perhaps the group had another purpose. After all, the play itself was not anti-American. It distinguished clearly between bad Americans, like the lynch mob and the sadistic state police captain, and good Americans, like the sheriff who pursues the pair without enthusiasm and even comes to feel sympathy for them. In fact, in showing the two convicts progressing from mutual hatred, to cooperation, to a denouement in which the Negro chooses to stay with his wounded comrade rather than escape, the play affirms a universal ideal of racial harmony. Were the Russians trying to convey this message? Were they even mindful of tensions, in their own orbit, between white and dark-skinned?

I didn't know what they had on their minds, but I was curious to find out. I agreed to attend further rehearsals without committing myself to work through to opening night.

I had heard rumors about Africans being mistreated in the Soviet Union; Russians themselves recounted the grisly one about the African who chased a Russian girl in Leningrad, was clubbed by Russian men, and left in a snow bank to freeze to death. Students I asked about the problem were eager to talk. They all deplored beatings and killings, whether in Philadelphia, Mississippi, or in Leningrad, and they condemned crude forms of segregation in buses, schools, housing, and jobs. But many said they recognized "the difficulties of dealing with *chiornye,*" and more than a few blithely made offensive generalizations that would have shocked all Americans except those who still talk the same way themselves.

"Africans are naturally less intelligent than whites."

"Blacks like to live in hot rooms, and they sweat more than whites."

"Blacks have the moral character of children."

Such a Russian once remarked knowingly, "You have twenty million of them, so you know, eh? No wonder you've got problems in the States."

And the nasty accusations were aimed not only at Africans. Asians, even Soviet Asians, were also occasional targets. I remember visiting a Russian in his *blok* and watching as a *tarakan*—cockroach—raced across his floor. My friend trampled it and muttered, only partly in jest, "What can you expect with an Uzbekh as a neighbor. He just got back from a vacation and must have brought the *tarakan* in his *chemodan* (suitcase)."

One evening I saw several cockroaches disporting themselves in my bathroom. Did that mean, in my friend's logic, that America deserved to take the rap?

A few Soviets grumbled that Africans had fat scholarships, fancy Western clothes, and expensive tastes in food and Russian women.

"Oppressed colonial masses, hell," said a Russian. "Half of them are tribal chiefs. No wonder some are disappointed here. They had it better back home."

These Russians complained that well-to-do Africans disdained the long *stolovaia* lines and browbeat white waitresses. But Russians, and Americans, too, were occasionally guilty of these sins. Some Russians pointed out with a smirk that Africans stood around staring at Soviet girls. But didn't we all?

It is true that Africans at MGU remained apart. Was it because Russians rebuffed them? Or were they fearful of being rebuffed? Many Russians went out of their way to be hospitable and invited the Africans to parties and dances in the dormitory lounges. But other Russians threw stones through the lounge window during an integrated dance. "Were the students under the influence of vodka when they threw the stones?" I asked. "No," I was told. "They were just feeling frisky."

Russians I met away from the university—waitresses, workers, and taxi drivers for example—would also bring up the subject of the racial discrimination.

Some said, Shame on America. But a few, who sounded like bigoted Americans, cursed the African visitation.

Despite the lofty principles of Communism and the guarantees of its constitution, the Soviet Union has its share of racial prejudice. I must say I was surprised to find it at the university. Indeed, I gathered the impression, which I cannot support with statistics, that there is more fierce dedication to the idea of equality among races at places like Harvard and Columbia than at MGU.

The members of the International Student Theater did believe passionately in brotherhood. Although they didn't put it into words, I could sense it at the first rehearsals. They were more than patient with their recruit from the Cameroons, who stumbled constantly over the rocks of Russian language. They tried hard to understand the American characters they were playing. When there were rumors that a high official of the *Dom Kul'tury* was considering canceling the production because he feared a clash between whites and blacks in the audience, the troupe did not turn back. Watching them at work I became convinced of their good faith, and I began to spend more time trying to help them.

As a Northerner, I didn't pretend to be an expert on the South. But I didn't need to be one to know that a deerstalker's hat à la Sherlock Holmes was not suitable headgear for the sheriff. I suggested a broad-brimmed hat, and the wardrobe mistress smilingly produced a floppy *shliapa*—hat—that Khrushchev might have worn on his American safari. I showed a copy of *Life* to the designer and she based her costumes on its pictures of Alabama state troopers. They worried about troopers' boots until I assured them that Red Army boots would do. I brought in gum for the deputies to chew, and suggested that those in the lynch mob nibble now and then on blades of grass. The director asked whether the Russians weren't playing too somberly. "Wouldn't Americans laugh more, even while chasing escaped convicts?" I said I thought they probably would.

But all their arduous efforts and good will, and my advice, such as it was, availed them not. The production was a flop. Why? The translation of the screenplay into a play didn't work. The African's stilted Russian didn't help; the audience laughed instead of shuddering when he spit out the servile words: *"Slushaiu boss. Slushaiu boss. Slushaiu boss.* (I'm listenin', boss)." And students said they stayed away because they had recently seen the film.

The group was disappointed and met to ponder these questions: What was the studio's purpose? What did its members want from it? Were they willing to work for it? Should members study theater in class, or should they simply work on presenting plays? Were they capable of disciplining themselves, or should the director be tougher? It was agreed, in the end, that the best answer to all these questions would be an exciting play.

But what play?

"Rhinoceros, by Ionesco," someone called out.

The suggestion seemed to catch everyone's imagination. Was it that *Rhinoceros* would be controversial? In the past the plays of Ionesco, like those of Beckett and Pinter, have not been welcome in the Soviet Union. They have been regarded officially as reflections of capitalist society and its supposed breakdown in human communication. Soviet audiences, one has been told, would find nothing recognizable in them and would not like them. I was astonished that any Russians would contemplate doing any play by Ionesco. I assumed they were well aware of the official attitude, and yet they were excited about the prospect and seemed to think that they could do the play if they wanted to. They pointed out that the monthly periodical, *Inostrannaia Literatura,* had recently printed a Russian translation of *Rhinoceros*—that's where they had read it. As if to dramatize the point, two members stood up and waved copies.

A lively discussion developed. One chap warned that the play's ridiculing of the herd instinct could be interpreted as a travesty of Communist collectivism. Another scoffed at this notion, arguing that Ionesco was lambasting the bourgeoisie. Someone else insisted that the target was really the fascist herd.

"There are good herds and bad herds," he said.

"It depends on where the herd is running," put in a girl in the group.

"What really matters," said another man, "is that *Inostrannaia Literatura* has printed it. That means there would be no obstacle to staging it."

"But are we good enough to do the play?" asked another member.

Someone else offered another suggestion—a play about Molière by a playwright named Mikhail Bulgakov. This one, he said, dealt with the place of an artist in a dictatorial state.

"It was produced in 1936," he added. "But it was quickly withdrawn. For obvious reasons."

I never learned how the issue was resolved. Before any decision was reached, my time in the Soviet Union was up. If they did either play, I should have liked to see it.

My guitar brought me into contact with another extracurricular cultural *kollektiv.* A committee of law students asked me to take part in a Juridical Faculty performance, its entry in a competition among all the MGU faculties. Each year, the students and teachers of each faculty present a playlet and a concert. A jury of thirty-five professional performers, directors, and critics picks the best playlet and nominates individual students to repeat their acts in a final all–MGU concert.

The committee of students preparing the Juridical Faculty's production wanted me for the playlet and the concert. My duties at the concert would be simple: I would sing several American folk songs alone. But the playlet was the thing that almost caught the conscience of an American and of some Russians, too. The plot of the skit revolved around secret agent James Bond, 007 himself, whose exploits have not appeared in translation in the Soviet Union because, according to the Soviet press, he is a fascist figure symbolizing the cruelty and amorality of the West. In the playlet, Bond was supposed to penetrate the MGU Juridical Faculty, only to find that the daily work load and the intricacies of Soviet jurisprudence were too much for his Anglo-Saxon mind. As the curtain fell, he was to flunk out ignominiously.

The student directors of this tragicomic tale wanted me to sing "The Midnight Special" in the background while Bond's chief gave him his final instructions. I told the directors that an American chain gang song didn't make much sense in the London headquarters of the Secret Service. But they, who had never been to England or America, seemed to get a boot out of the idea and were reluctant to let go. Several Russians in the cast were embarrassed, however. "How can you ask an American to sing an American song in an anti-NATO skit?" one asked. But since the skit was pure farce, I agreed to do it.

In the end my virtue was rewarded, for the playlet closed on the road. The first full rehearsal didn't take place until the day before opening night, and the directors somehow couldn't shape it up by curtain time. Losing the playlet meant losing points in the competition, and so, with a heavy heart, the Juridical Faculty presented only its concert.

The concert artists were an odd and exuberant lot. A dance group performed à la Moiseyev. A tenor who resembled Robert Goulet and had the same effect on the girls sang "*Rodina* (Motherland)." A chorus sang Russian folk songs. An old, old man, said to be the last specialist on Roman law extant in the U.S.S.R., offered a piano sonata. A slightly younger professor of criminal law played a slightly squeaky violin. A swinging exchange student from the Congo jived all over the stage in tight trousers and a snazzy blue blazer belting out the latest Paris hits in French. A Russian jazz combo played American Dixieland as well as some Russian numbers. And a Soviet student, dressed to look like an elderly professor in false eyebrows and mustache, offered a roguish monologue, a Marxist interpretation of "The Role of the Cloakroom in History." He reminded me more of Groucho Marx than of Karl.

Then it was my turn. The *Dom Kul'tury* auditorium was filled with students, professors, and jury. I stood backstage and listened to the master of ceremonies introducing me.

"We present American folk songs performed by a student of the Juridical Faculty."

The curtain opened, I stepped forward into the spotlight and was greeted, even before I opened my mouth, with one of the loudest cheers of the night. I introduced my first number in Russian.

"It is called 'John Henry.' John Henry was a Negro slave who worked on the railroad. He was a strong, proud man, and when the boss demanded impossible work, John Henry didn't refuse to do it. John Henry died on the railroad and his story became a legend."

The audience responded warmly to "John Henry," as it did to my second number, a rock-and-roll ballad called "Woe Woe Woe," which I had written with my brother Philip. My third and last song was "We Shall Overcome," which the concert committee had insisted I sing. I had taught the words to members of the Faculty chorus and I invited them and the audience to sing along. *"My pobedim*—We shall overcome; *My budem khodit' ruka v ruke*—We'll walk hand in hand; *My budem zhit' mirno*—We shall live in peace." It sounded to me as if more than half the hall was singing.

The Juridical Faculty finished well down in the competition, but the jury awarded me a top score of ten and nominated me for the all-MGU finals. After the concert my friends congratulated me in the lobby. "You are the best propaganda America has," one professor said somewhat dramatically.

The Russians had more confidence in me than I had. Without false modesty, let me be objective. I am not that good. I was briefly in a folk music trio at college, but I had no illusion that my performance merited the cheers. What the Russians were expressing, I thought, was their warm feeling toward America.

But what was being expressed when I was not informed of the date of the all-MGU concert, so that I missed it and did not perform after all? Here was the sad sequence of events: A rehearsal was scheduled for Thursday and the concert for the following Monday. When I arrived Thursday to rehearse I was told that the session was postponed until Friday. On Friday I was notified that "the concert has been postponed indefinitely."

"Please tell me when you schedule it again," I requested. But the next Tuesday, when I still hadn't heard, I decided to check.

"The concert was held last night," I was told by a woman working in the *Dom Kul'tury*. "When you didn't come, we assumed you didn't want to appear."

The truth was exactly the opposite. I wanted very much to appear, but no one had advised me that the concert would take place on Monday night after all. The woman was apologetic and apparently chagrined. "It was a terrible mix-up," she said.

I would have been more inclined to buy that explanation if I hadn't seen some anti-American "Vietnam" posters in a room backstage. Had they been displayed during the concert? If not, was it embarrassing anyway to listen to and perhaps applaud an American in these troubled times?

"You must believe me," said the woman anticipating my doubts. "There was absolutely nothing political involved in this. Nothing at all. It was just a human bureaucratic misunderstanding."

Clearly she was distressed. Obviously she believed what she said. I didn't know what to think. Later I talked to the committeemen at the Juridical Faculty who had been assigned to notify me of the final concert. They, too, were apologetic. Each man said he had thought the other was letting me know.

Whatever the true explanation, the authorities tried to make it up to me. They invited me to a special concert in honor of those who performed at the all-MGU show. They presented me with gifts of a mechanical pencil and stationery.

A short time before I was to leave the Soviet Union, an official of the *Dom Kul'tury* approached me with a suggestion. The best performers from the all-MGU competition were going to tour the Soviet Union that summer. How would I like to join them with my American folk songs? I said I would be delighted, but that in accordance with the exchange program schedule, I was supposed to leave the country in early summer. I had reason to believe that extensions of stay were difficult to get, except for urgent academic reasons. But if the *Dom Kul'tury* could arrange it, I said, I would be happy to stay. I did not hear from him again. I assumed that he could not arrange it.

13

A Taste for the New

ALTHOUGH it took some time before I began to appreciate the subtleties and differences in student taste, I was struck immediately by the great interest of nearly all my Soviet friends and acquaintances in theater, films, music, books, and art—in all matters artistic and intellectual. Not just the specialists in literature and art, but students from all faculties prided themselves on being *au courant* with the latest developments and trends. And a lightning-like word of mouth kept everyone informed of what was *interesno* and worth investigating. Although stipends were not large, books and tickets were cheap. Perhaps the most expensive ticket in town, a ticket to the *Bol'shoi,* cost three rubles; and the lowest-priced ticket to movies in the dorm was only twenty kopecks. With tickets so reasonable, there was no need for special student rates.

Anyone familiar with great American universities, especially those not in the center of large cities, knows how many enticing events, from lectures to full symphony orchestras, compete for students' and faculty's spare time. MGU, I would say, had more going on than most American universities. In part this is probably because the university is on the outskirts of the city; but in larger measure, this cornucopia of attractions was the response to a tremendous demand from the university population.

Toward the end of each month, large poster-like calendars went up in the lobby listing events of the coming month. Later more large posters advertised each attraction again. There were concerts by professionals, by orchestras like the Moscow State Symphony and the Philharmonic conducted by Kiril Kondrashin and David Oistrakh, with soloists like Emil Gilels and Igor Oistrakh.

There were *estradnye konsterty* or vaudeville-like stage shows featuring professional music hall entertainers: comedians, crooners, dancers, jugglers, and puppet acts.

There were poetry readings, illustrated lectures about foreign countries, combined lecture-concerts on musical subjects, special orations by distinguished scholars, and question and answer sessions with experts entitled "You ask—We answer Oral Journals."

Amateur events included performances by MGU groups—dance studios, pantomime theater and chorus—and by student troupes from Communist countries of East Europe. There were also occasional exhibitions of works by student artists. And upstairs in the dormitory lounges small groups arranged special evenings to which the public was invited. I accepted the invitation of a hastily scribbled poster in the lobby and found a surprisingly large turnout listening to a recording of Handel's *Messiah.* Another club called Friends of the Films invited students to discuss the latest movies.

The latest movies played almost every night at MGU, and even a casual observer could tell which films fired the students' imagination. When a good one was showing, a long line began forming at the box office two or three hours before starting time. Then, just before the showing, students stalked the lobby trying to buy *lishnye bilety*—extra tickets. When the demand for *lishnye* was particularly great, last minute buyers took up positions far from the auditorium hoping to buttonhole prospective sellers before they reached the crowded lobby. When I got the hang of things, I formulated what might be called the "MGU Film Law:" The greater the distance between the theater and the seekers of *lishnye bilety*, the better the picture.

Films from the West drew extraordinary crowds. Students mobbed Stanley Kramer's *Judgment at Nuremburg* and *The Defiant Ones*. They loved his *Bezumnyi Bezumnyi Bezumnyi Mir* (*It's a Mad Mad Mad World*). They packed the house for the British comedy *Carry on Nurse* on the very night when a Soviet documentary about the Russian Civil War attracted only a dozen viewers, including me. They admired French films like *Sundays and Cybèle* and Italian pictures like *Divorce—Italian Style* and *Marriage—Italian Style*. The latter, in fact, was voted the second most popular film in a 1965 Soviet popularity poll, just behind a Soviet movie called *The Chairman*.

When MGU arranged a special showing of Michaelangelo Antonioni's *L'Avventura*, admission was by invitation only, apparently because the sponsors feared that publicity would attract an unmanageable mob. But as soon as ticket holders began to arrive, the word began to spread, and before long the lobby was clogged with an unmanageable mob after all. Some students struggled in without invitations; others with tickets could not get in. Afterwards many wondered whether the film had been worth the struggle, whether it was profound or just plain *skuchno*—dull. Another event that was kept quiet and yet drew an S.R.O. crowd was a concert by the American folk singer Pete Seeger.

Russians were just as curious about Western films they could not see, films the Soviet government chose not to import. Among these were spy stories, gangster pictures, and westerns.

"I guess I understand why James Bond is out of the

question," said a student sadly. "We can't very well spend our scarce foreign exchange to import anti-Soviet propaganda. But why not show American movies about crime? After all, they make good anti-American propaganda." My friend paused and an ironic smile played across his face. "Our newspapers are always crowing about the increase in crime in America. They tell us that you're no longer safe on the streets at night. Well, why not show us some gangster pictures so we can see for ourselves just how bad things are?"

"I'll tell you why not," replied a movie buff at the Juridical Faculty. "We have enough trouble with *hooligany* without giving them more bad examples to imitate. Show them gangsters or cowboys and Indians and they start to play the parts in real life. The country is still getting over the shock caused by the American western called *The Magnificent Seven.* That film ensured the eternal popularity of blue jeans in the U.S.S.R. The cultural bureaucrats learned their lesson on that one."

The thirst for films from the West was so great that I wondered for awhile whether it wasn't indiscriminate and uncritical. But there was evidence to indicate that most students were thoughtful and discerning in their choices. They didn't storm the gates to an old Mario Lanza musical, and few liked *Desire Under the Elms* despite the presence in it of Sophia Loren, whose physical endowments appeal to Russians as much as to Americans, Italians, and probably, if they got the chance, to the Chinese Red Guards. Some of my friends recalled wistfully that they had failed to see *West Side Story* when it was shown briefly at a film festival in Moscow. But no one took the trouble to attend a dull production of *West Side Story* by the MGU Pantomime Theater which, for some unfathomable reason, used not Leonard Bernstein's score, but a hodgepodge consisting mainly of Gershwin's music from *Porgy and Bess. One Potato, Two Potato,* the American film dealing with a racial problem, attracted small crowds and less admiration. The complaint was that the film was melodramatic and preachy.

"It reminds me of socialist realism," said a student contemptuously.

"We're tired of message films," said another.

The truth was that they were not at all tired of message films when they admired the message. They liked Soviet director Mikhail Romm's documentary study of *Ordinary Fascism* and professed to see a double meaning in it. On the surface it was a dissection of Nazism, but Russians saw in it a sermon, by analogy, on the evils of Stalinism.

I was fascinated by MGU audience reaction to *The Chairman,* the 1965 film popularity poll winner. The picture tells the story of a ruggedly honest collective farm chairman who, in the last years of Stalin's rule, bucked Party hacks, even though he accepted the Party's ideals. The audience cheered when rank-and-file farmers rose up to rebuff an arrogant Party secretary, and it burst into applause again when the death of Stalin was announced on the screen.

I told a Russian friend, a graduate student in the Juridical Faculty, that the picture was impressive and so was the response of students, who seemed champions of the outspoken film.

"You may be right about the students," he replied. "But you're a little naïve about the film. It's not that outspoken. Sure, the chairman fought the Party hacks and won. But to me he isn't a convincing character. He is a superman, too perfect to be true. That kind of clean, tough, honest, intelligent figure is a wild exaggeration, just as false as the noble tractor-driving heroes of old. As Khrushchev used to say, 'Life is complex, *tovarshchi.*' In real life, heroes have weaknesses. Furthermore, the film is flawed because it assumes that the battle ended in 1953 when Stalin died. That's where the film compromised. That's why even Khrushchev could like it."

My friends liked a Soviet film called *Thirty-Three* which they said was a first of its kind. A mad farce about a simple factory worker who is made a national hero because he has thirty-three teeth instead of the normal thirty-two, *Thirty-Three* had some of the fast-moving inventive exuberance of *The Knack,* and its hero was nearly as dim-witted as Stan Laurel. But since it twitted the national adulation of cosmonauts more than the personality cult, I was surprised to hear a rumor that the film was in trouble with the censor. True or not, the gossip only made my Russian colleagues more anxious to see it.

"Of course it's not devastating satire," admitted a student of economics. "But at least it laughs at organized spontaneity. And even if it were pure froth, what's wrong with that? It's a good change from dull didactic stuff."

After awhile I began to think that I could predict student reaction. They liked daring films that criticized political shibboleths, and they were fond of apolitical films that concentrated on homely human problems. They disliked films crudely designed for uplift. Movies about heroic workers, cranes, and hoists, I thought, could no longer rouse my friends.

But I was wrong. *Time Forward* was a new movie about production heroics at a cement factory in the 1930's, about young workers on a Komsomol brigade who expend superhuman efforts to overfulfill their Plan and win a competition with other factories. I thought the film, based on Valentine Kataev's 1932 novel, was optimistic in the most slushy way, and I assumed that my friends would agree. But the very men and women who snickered when the radio hailed similar production feats, were stirred. It took them back, they said, to a time when an earlier Soviet generation was certain it could build a new world overnight and went out with picks and shovels to prove it. My friends didn't say it, but I thought they looked back longingly to the days before the Great

Purges and the Great War, when young people had fewer doubts, higher hopes, and more illusions.

When it came to the theater, a play about the very first days of the Revolution was a prime favorite. The Drama and Comedy Theater's adaptation of John Reed's *Ten Days That Shook the World* looked back with pride and nostalgia and went to ingenious lengths to make the spectator feel, from the moment he entered the lobby, the excitement of 1917. Ushers dressed as Revolutionary sailors in long greatcoats and red bandannas impaled ticket stubs on their bayonets. Usherettes pinned red flowers of the Revolution on lapels of theatergoers. The production was just as vivid and imaginative, and students came home glowing.

But wasn't the play's message hackneyed? I asked. Even though the portraits of gallant proletarians and evil bourgeoisie were stylized and had flashes of humor, weren't they the same old stereotypes?

"Of course they were," replied a student of history whom I had taken to be an enemy of all clichés. "But who cares, if they're well done? Nobody insists that every play or every film must beat its breast, or unmask hypocrisy, or reveal a true and telling slice of life. There's nothing wrong with waving the flag and celebrating the Revolution if you do it with style and imagination."

It was only natural that students responded to the Drama and Comedy Theater on Taganka, for this troupe is the youngest in Moscow. It was formed a few years ago when Yuri Liubimov, a veteran actor of the Vakhtangov Theater, created a student production of Brecht's *Good Woman of Setzuan,* which was so good that the group was invited to move into the theater on Taganka. Among this company's other productions favored by the students were *Antiworlds,* from the poetry of Andrei Voznesenky, who with Yevtushenko has become virtually a spokesman for the younger Soviet generation, and *The Caucasian Chalk Circle* by

Brecht, who has only lately been admitted to the Soviet stage.

Like nearly everyone in Moscow I wanted to see Taganka troupe's productions, but I rarely succeeded. If you didn't get in the line early, or know someone, you were out of luck. Tourists are in a better position to get scarce *bilety,* because a proportion of tickets to nearly all attractions is held for them by Intourist, the official travel agency, which supervises foreign tourists. But being an American was no help to me. I was treated like all other students.

The *Sovremennik* Theater—The Contemporary—was just as popular. One of the productions students most admired was a revival of Evgeni Shvarts' *The Naked King,* a play that does not wave the flag at all. On the contrary, although the story takes place in a make-believe kingdom and mocks a make-believe court, the play, according to its admirers, was on Soviet target. Written in 1934, *The Naked King* has been officially hailed as an attack on Hitler, but my friends, who were anxious for me to see it and briefed me on allusions to watch for, had Stalin in mind. The story takes off from Hans Christian Andersen's "The Emperor's New Clothes," but in the realm of Shvarts' Emperor, the king is a fierce tyrant, his subjects are forced to genuflect, anyone who dissents is shot on the spot, and even romance is regimented by a Ministry of Love. I thought I caught most of the contemporary references, but afterwards students took pains to debrief me, to make sure I had not missed any.

Had it struck me, someone asked, how timely the play was? I hesitantly answered, "Are you thinking of Sinyavsky and Daniel?" He nodded. We both understood what was meant. Sinyavsky and Daniel stood accused of slandering the Soviet people. One of the questions fired at them was, If you did not mean to slander the Soviet Union, why did you place their stories in a Soviet setting? Why didn't you set them in some make-believe kingdom? We didn't discuss the subject further, but I thought to myself that if *The Naked King* took place in a contemporary Soviet setting, it never would have seen the light of day. In fact, for years, the play was neither performed or published in the Soviet Union.

When I got to know Russians well enough, I raised the question of the limits of permissible criticism. I was referred by students to a favorite play of theirs, *Tiorkin in the Other World,* by Alexander Tvardovsky, at the Theater of Satire. Tiorkin is the soldier innocent who discovers that heaven, too, is divided into two camps by a cold war, that his camp is tightly controlled, and that if he crawls on his belly up to the wall he can hear enough Ella Fitzgerald and Louis Armstrong on the other side to set his toes to tapping and his hands to clapping. When I saw the play, Tvardovsky's journal *Novy Mir* had recently come under attack at the Party Congress, and he had lost his membership on the Party's Central Committee. But when one of the actors held up a copy of *Novy Mir* and mentioned "the author of our play," the audience stood and cheered.

If the critical tone of *Tiorkin* was heady stuff to students, and the rousing patriotism of *Ten Days* was fun, there were also apolitical plays that my friends admired—for example, Edward Radzinsky's *104 Pages About Love,* at a theater that bears the thoroughly political name of Theater of the Leninskii Komsomol. *104 Pages About Love* presents characters with whom young people can readily identify. It is the story of an uneven love affair between a young scientist and an airline stewardess; she loves him a lot; he is drawn to her but pulls back because he considers her beneath his station. Coming to the noble conclusion that she is not bright enough for him, she gives him up, and then, in an air disaster, she gives up her own life to save others. In the end the young hero knows that he has suffered an irretrievable loss.

I told a friend that I thought too many of the *104 Pages* lachrymose.

"You may be right," replied my friend, who had told me

he was a member of the Party. "But you have to admit there's no propaganda in the play. Why, the Communist Party is not mentioned at all."

Alexei Arbuzov's *The Irkutsk Story* must have seemed remarkably clear of cant when first produced, not too long ago. But it was already considered old-fashioned. Telling of young people working at a Siberian construction sight, it eschews political clichés until the climax. But the climax was what some couldn't take. The hero dies trying to save a drowning boy and leaves his wife and friends desolate. She, after a period of darkest depression, announces she will overcome her grief by devoting herself to work, to the building of Communism. Her husband's colleagues console themselves by picturing the future: "What remains after the death of a workingman? His work. His work remains forever. Under Communism there will be no such thing as death because a man's work will be a hundred times finer than today."

"That line is too much," complained a student heatedly. "Of course, they're right that you have to go on living. But why do they make ideological speeches about it?"

Russians love Chekhov, but some students said they were tired of the Moscow Art Theater's old-fashioned productions. To them, the Leninskii Komsomol Theater's modern staging of *The Seagull,* with its allusive stylized settings, was far more interesting. They admired the production even though they thought that director Anatoli Efros' experiments in the last act began to get in the way.

The theater of the absurd was a subject many at MGU asked about. They had no chance to see examples on their own stage and had little opportunity to read the works. Those who followed the Moscow theater closely were angry and ashamed when it turned out they knew little of Beckett, Pinter, and Genet. But there has been some liberalization. *Inostrannaia Literatura,* the periodical that first published

Ionesco's *Rhinoceros,* recently ran a Russian translation of Beckett's *Waiting for Godot.*

Regular theatergoers considered Brecht the most far-out playwright in town and rejoiced that he was being produced in several Moscow theaters. At MGU, the downtown theater studio presented a student production of *Arturo Ui* which drew full houses week after week and had to extend its run. Clearly Brecht had a solid student following, but some Russians had reservations.

"The interesting thing about Brecht is the form of his plays," observed a law student who was a theater buff. "But the content is not new at all. In fact, the message is familiar."

American novels were a source of fascination to the students. Salinger, long a favorite, was already somewhat passé among the *filologi* (literally philologists; actually students studying literature in the Philology Faculty). They were even indifferent, it seemed, to a stage version of Salinger's *Catcher in the Rye* at the Theater of Satire. Experts like these wanted as much information as I could give them about Saul Bellow, John Updike, and Philip Roth. Several confided that they would like to translate these authors, and asked me to help them obtain copies of the books.

Among Soviet authors, Vasili Aksionov remained a great favorite. Several times students groping to find words to sum up the mood of the younger generation referred me to the cool teen-age heroes of Aksionov's 1961 classic *Starry Ticket.*

Alexander Solzhenitsin, author of *One Day in the Life of Ivan Denisovitch,* is apparently a hero to many, and his right to speak his mind in print was rapidly becoming a cause célèbre at MGU. Important Party critics have attacked Solzhenitsin for concentrating on the evils of Stalin's purges and prison camps. They would prefer a balanced treatment of the past, stressing positive achievements. Students, however, were not convinced by this argument, as I was to discover at a hotly contested meeting of students and Party experts.

Among the poets, Yevtushenko was respected by my Russian friends for his outspoken criticism, but they were not so eager to rush to his defense. Yevtushenko could take care of himself, they said, in a way that was not altogether complimentary. They accused him of arrogance. Symptomatic of their love-hate attitude was their reaction to his poem *Letter to Yesenin*. The poem had not been published, but typewritten copies were passed from hand to hand at MGU and each student who saw it made his own copy to keep. The poem contained a direct attack on the leader of the Komsomol, as a friend who was a Komsomol member pointed out to me. My friend was not in the least distressed; in fact he was chortling. I quote from the poem, which has been published in the United States in a translation by George Reavey:

When the ruddy-faced Komsomol chief
Crashes his fist against us poets,
And wants to work our minds like wax,
And wants to shape us to look like him,

His words, Yesenin, are not frightening,
But neither do they make one happy . . .
For I, believe me, don't feel like running
With rolled up breeches behind this Komsomol.

My Komsomol within whose ranks I march,
Is building up Bratsk and planting in the Altai.
My Komsomol, after whom I want to run
Is you—Pushkin, Mayakovsky and Yesenin.

My friend, who obviously agreed with Yevtushenko, could not stomach the poet's placing himself in the immortal company of Pushkin, Mayakovksy, and Yesenin.

"That kind of arrogance is not needed," he said. "It's irrelevant and distracting. It gives his enemies a chance to say that he is an egotist. It contributes nothing to the cause."

Of the poems that circulated underground at MGU, I

remember an anonymous one, a hilarious parody of Pushkin's *Bronze Horseman* with Nikita Khrushchev cast, in perfect meter and rhyme, as the hero. The same Russian who carped at *Letter to Yesenin* thought this one was needed and contributed to the cause, and he endorsed it without reservation.

Satire was big at MGU. The marvelously funny stories of Ilf and Petrov were back in fashion, if indeed they were ever out of fashion. And if there was one actor-entertainer whom students adored above all others, it was the satirist Arkadi Raikin. A man who writes like James Thurber and speaks like Danny Kaye, Raikin runs a Theater of Miniatures in Leningrad and occasionally visits Moscow to do an evening of monologues. When he came to MGU, more than a thousand students waited in long lines for tickets and then waited impatiently for two hours in the hot *Aktovyi Zal* while other acts preceded him. After Raikin had appeared, they pleaded for more and more encores and refused to leave the hall. I was lucky enough to get a ticket and I was astonished at the impudence of his sallies. He worked without props or special costumes and managed to make every vignette real. As a father viewing infants in a nursery, he suddenly stood back in puzzlement. "How do they," he paused meaningfully, "How do they make demagogues out of these babies?" In another scene he did a hilarious job on bureaucrats. Playing several characters at once, he depicted fire department officials dithering fatuously over red tape while a frantic woman's house burned down.

To an American, Raikin's thrusts seemed pointed, but good-humored. I found, however, that some Russians are extra sensitive to even this kind of satire. A Soviet friend told me he would not have been surprised if the fire department had squawked about Raikin. He recalled that taxi drivers had complained publicly that an irreverent description of one cabbie was an insult to the entire profession. Unhappy cab drivers could be laughed off, my friend went on, but it was not so easy to dismiss the objections of highly placed critics who argue that it is more constructive to teach people how to improve than to ridicule them. He remembered an article in *Izvestia* in which Raikin himself took on the humorless critics, contending that the way to get people to improve was to point out their weaknesses.

"The whole debate is ridiculous," said my friend. "To think that we have to make solemn speeches in defense of satire. Don't those who protest realize that they are more ludicrous than any satirist's caricature?"

When we discussed painting, sculpture, and architecture, I discovered that virtually none of my friends worshiped at the shrine of old style socialist realism, that photo-like images of *kolkhozniks,* tractors, and cranes left them cold. My friends welcomed modern techniques and experimentation, at least in principle. They reported that some old taboos were disappearing, and they were glad to see them go. They applauded the Ministry of Culture's decision to exhibit the painting of Alexander Tishler at the Pushkin Museum, even though the artist's work had been attacked in the past for being too modernist. Attending the huge exhibition at Manezh of the Art of the Baltic Republics (Latvia, Lithuania, and Estonia), they hailed the timid tries at abstractionism and were disappointed that they didn't go very far. Some physics students told me proudly that a Physics Institute in Moscow was showing the works of unorthodox artists still under attack from conservatives in the Union of Soviet Artists. One evening, as a number of us sat around in the dorm, a foreign student passed around a book on Jackson Pollack that contained colored illustrations. Immediately there was a sharp division of opinion.

"A man like that could become a new God," said a literature *studentka* who prided herself on her receptivity to new ideas.

But a history student, who would have said his taste was equally emancipated, followed the conservative line. "I didn't realize we were fighting for freedom for stuff like this. If that's the case, perhaps we should slow down a little."

I don't mean to say that Soviet students spent all their time weighing the political nuances of plays and films and books and looking for new waves to ride in art. They could sit back and enjoy the ballet and the opera. They could follow the fortunes of young pianists in the Tchaikovsky contests as Americans might follow baseball players fighting to win a batting championship. They could fill the *Aktovyi Zal* at MGU for Gilels and Oistrakh playing Beethoven and Tchaikovsky. They could laugh at a play like Leonid Zorin's *Encyclopedists,* which pokes fun at provincial intelligentsia in such an exaggerated way that it becomes, like a Kaufman-Hart creation, pure farce. And they could enjoy *estradnye kontserty* featuring some of the most cornball acts I have ever seen. I could hardly believe it when an MGU audience roared its approval of a short, fat, and balding crooner dressed in a white sheepskin jacket, tasseled trousers, earrings, and elevator shoes, who was accompanied by three strolling violinists with sobbing strings. And I was shocked when physics students who seemed otherwise sophisticated melted at the mawkish television tribute to Soviet women on the eve of International Woman's Day. Then I remembered that most Soviet tourists I have guided around New York have insisted on a visit to Radio City Music Hall.

Obviously the films shown, the plays produced, the books available, and the works of art on open exhibit in Moscow are tolerated if not actively and enthusiastically endorsed by the Party. But as has been reported in the West, there is a considerable amount of underground literature and art—typewritten and mimeographed copies of poems and stories that circulate quietly and privately, and exhibitions that take place off the beaten art path without any publicity. I assumed that this was a delicate subject, and when I first hesitantly broached it to a Russian student I expected him to disclaim any knowledge of it. Instead, my friend, a Party member himself, plunged right in.

"Let's not be naïve. Of course there's a lot of underground art and literature. Everybody knows it, and everybody knows that it includes the work of established figures as well as outcasts. Writers like Solzhenitsin, Okudzhava, and even Yevtushenko don't have all their work published immediately. Some of it has to get around privately. The people on top, who could put a stop to it, know all about it. And if they're willing to put up with it, that's probably because they think it gives intellectuals a chance to let off steam. They know that artists have to show their work to someone. Of course, when things get too annoying, the authorities can and do crack down."

What was puzzling was suppression that seemed to make no sense. We heard at MGU that a production of Arthur Miller's *Incident at Vichy* had been rehearsed and was ready to open at one of Moscow's leading theaters—but it couldn't get approval from on high. I couldn't understand why, and when I summed up the play's content for a few of my Russian friends, they were equally bewildered. One, however, proposed possible reasons.

"Could it be that it could be uncomfortable to be reminded that we sat and did nothing to fight Nazism for nearly two years after the Nazi-Soviet Pact? And it might be unpleasant to raise the issue of men's responsibility to oppose a dictator and the guilt of those who don't. After all, we once had a little experience with a dictator ourselves."

It is no news that there is no such thing as complete freedom for artists and writers in the Soviet Union. But as far as my friends at MGU were concerned, there was too much freedom for works they regarded as trite and embarrassing. They pointed to writing in *Oktiabr,* the mouthpiece of the conservative literary wing, which they called at best banal, and to the most hackneyed examples of didactic painting. In the West these would be called camp. In the Soviet Union they are still taken seriously and their worth is hotly debated. But students have begun to laugh at them, indicating that the day is fast approaching when a masterpiece of socialist realism may be viewed in the Soviet Union, too, as a classic in reverse. The noble Stakhanovite hero of old may yet become the Batman of a mature Soviet culture.

Symptomatic of young people's sophistication is their eagerness for contact with all sorts of developments in the West, including those that the Communist Party does not welcome in the Soviet Union. Equally significant is their support for what is new and daring and imaginative in underground art and literature. But in noting this some Western observers leave out of consideration a vital point: There is a great deal that sophisticated young Russians admire enormously in what is open and available in Moscow, as I found among my friends at MGU. Some of it is explicitly, if moderately, critical, like Tvardovsky's *Tiorkin* and Shvarts' *Naked King*. But other works, like *Ten Days,* openly glorify Communism and country. The tendency of some glib Western observers to read into these preferences strong commitments for or against the Party and government is a dangerous oversimplification. The truth is more complicated. Russians I got to know well, found no contradiction in being both critical of what they disliked and proud of what they admired.

"Who is the Party and who is the Komsomol?" said one. "Party officials attack Tvardovsky, but Tvardovsky too is a Party member and so are the students who cheer his critical play. The head of the Komsomol attacks Yevtushenko, but Yevtushenko also represents the Komsomol and so do millions of young people who admire his poetry."

I refrained from saying that the balance my friend drew was unequal, that if Tvardovsky and Yevtushenko could speak out, people with infinitely more power not only could speak out against them but suppress them as well.

14

As They See Us

THE interest of Soviet students in all things American was a constant source of wonder to me. They were curious about other Western countries, but the U.S.A. seemed to fascinate them most of all. Was I getting a distorted impression because Russians naturally addressed their questions about the U.S.A. to an American? When I sat in on public meetings devoted to life in foreign countries, I got the same impression. The best-attended meeting of all was one at which a *Pravda* correspondent described his years in the United States.

Which Russians were fascinated by the U.S.A.? I can only judge by those I knew, whether intimately or casually, but they represented a wide spectrum of backgrounds and interests. My friends and acquaintances at MGU studied in various faculties: Juridical, Economics, History, Philology, Philosophy, Journalism, Physics, Chemistry, and Mathematics. Some were freshmen and sophomores, most were in their third, fourth, or fifth years, and a few were graduate students. Some lived with their families in Moscow, but most hailed from smaller cities and towns in other parts of the U.S.S.R. A few had traveled outside the Soviet Union, but only to

Communist states of East Europe—on vacation, in student delegations, or in the armed forces. Virtually none of my friends had visited West Europe and no one had been to America.

The average age of the group was in the early twenties. No one had any personal recollection of the period of the Purges; a few had memories of the time of World War II. Many had served in the armed forces; others had worked in factories and laboratories after finishing high school.

I learned very little about my friends' families. Unlike Americans, Russians rarely ask, "What does your father do?" Students were more likely to ask, "Do you have parents?" A somber question, which revealed how many lost their lives in the war. As far as I knew, none of my friends were scions of famous Soviet families, though one or two told me they had fathers in relatively high Party places. Several said their fathers had been workers; others had been orphaned by the war.

As university students, my friends were automatically classed as members of the Soviet intelligentsia, and some, I would guess, will become distinguished intellectuals. But no one, as far as I knew, was a precocious novelist or poet. Nearly all read subterranean fiction and no doubt approved of it. But none, to my knowledge, belonged to any group or organized underground of discontented young intellectuals like the one called S.M.O.G. (in Russian the initials stand for "daring, thought, image, and profundity"), whose existence has been reported in the Western press.

Most of my friends were rank and file members of the Komsomol, a few were Komsomol leaders or activists, and several were members of the Communist Party itself. These political affiliations confirmed what other evidence suggested—that these were regarded officially as the nation's most promising young people. But with their favored positions came special responsibilities, and even among these there were differences in scope and weight. Party members, only a small fraction of the student body, were among the political elite of the university. They had won their memberships only after Party peers had testified to their loyalty and ability. And they had solemnly pledged to set an example for those outside the Party by actively supporting all the Party's goals and works.

The rank and file *komsomolets* did not live in such a rarified atmosphere, though the Party laid out as an ideal a set of duties that would have wafted him into the Communist empyrean. To read the Party's definition of the "main task" of the Komsomol, one would think that ordinary *komsomoltsy* at a place like MGU would be as dedicated as Party members are supposed to be. For that task, according to a Party handbook, was "to educate boys and girls in the heroic tradition of revolutionary struggle, in the examples of selfless labor of workers, collective farmers, and intelligentsia and in the great ideals of Marxism-Leninism; to prepare steadfast, highly educated, labor-loving young builders of Communism."

But obviously not all of the more than twenty-two million *komsomoltsy* between the ages of fourteen and twenty-eight live up to the ideal. MGU students readily admitted that they were not as heroic, selfless, steadfast, and labor-loving as the leaders of the Party and the Komsomol exhorted them to be. They had taken part, they said, in Komsomol activities; they had attended political and ideological lectures; they had volunteered to work in Komsomol construction brigades in Moscow and in the Virgin Lands; they had been tutors to the Young Pioneers, children in the national organization one step below the Komsomol; they had enjoyed Komsomol social activities—dances, athletics, excursions, amateur musical and theatrical productions. One Russian said he had even decided to vote on Election Day after a Komsomol activist came around to say, ominously, that the local Komsomol committee had heard he wasn't going to vote and wondered why. These *komsomoltsy* were content to remain rank-and-filers. "I am not an activist." I often heard that phrase from friends.

Those who earned the rank of Komsomol leaders were the activists. They were the elect who presumably measured up to the Komsomol ideal and would go on to join the Party.

Few Russians volunteered information about their political position. Was it possible to identify Party members, rank-and-file *komsomoltsy* and Komsomol activists by their behavior and opinions? Not nearly as easily as I had expected. Students who flaunted their knowledge of Western songs and begged for blue jeans were not Party members; the latter were too proud to carry on in this way, even if they felt like it. And those who consistently steered our conversations away from sensitive political questions often turned out to be Komsomol activists; some preferred not to get too chummy with an American; others assumed that we would quarrel about politics and feared to jeopardize our good relations. But a few activists and Party members spoke out more frankly and critically, even at their own government's expense, than ordinary *komsomoltsy* did, as if their rank gave them freedom and assurance.

Whatever the differences among these students, when it came to discussing America I had great difficulty in telling them apart. For virtually all, regardless of political position, were eager to ask about the U.S.A., and virtually no one resorted to stereotyped attacks.

Of course not all things American were potentially controversial. Take tea bags. I had purchased a package at the American Embassy Commissary, and they quickly caught my Soviet neighbors' fancy. Nearly everyone brewed hot tea on cold winter evenings, but the Russians brewed it loose in *chainiki* on the kitchen stoves. Tea bags, therefore, offered a short cut, and Russians who already knew and admired my

American cellophane tape and pencil sharpener asked to try this latest miracle. Before I could stop them, they had dumped the whole package, outer wrapper and all, into the hot water. But when I informed them that the Lipton people counted on their customers to remove the outer wrapper, the Russians' respect for American technology soared even higher.

"It made good tea, even with the wrapper on," a student reassured me, only half jokingly.

Residents of my floor asked me for academic aid. I helped a girl translate a chapter of *The Adventures of Tom Sawyer* into Russian in preparation for an English exam. I translated a *Pravda* editorial attacking U.S. imperialism into English for students who let me do all the work while they laughed and poked one another over the irony of the situation. In answer to a law student's question, I expounded the virtues of America's separation of powers, including the Supreme Court's right to declare unconstitutional acts of Congress. But, finishing my discourse, I began to worry that it had sounded propagandistic.

"We've got an organization that can annul acts of our highest legislative body, too," he said with a grin. "It's called the Communist Party."

When students asked about the look and price of American goods, I borrowed a Montgomery Ward catalogue from the American Embassy. The illustrations were more vivid than any words of mine, and if I didn't know the Russian word for a product we searched the catalogue for a picture of it. One student took the catalogue to a tailor and ordered a new suit to look like one in the book. The tailor, in turn, he reported, kept the catalogue to show the ads for ladies' underwear to his cronies. And the tailor's wife eventually took the magical volume away from the tailor to study photos of children's clothes. It was more than a month before I got the catalogue back. In the end I left it at MGU where, I suppose, it is still making the rounds.

Another American publication my friends were eager to see was *Amerika,* the colorful Russian language monthly of the United States Information Agency. *Amerika* is sold in the U.S.S.R. by virtue of the exchange agreement that authorized the Soviet government to offer its English language monthly, *Soviet Life,* in the United States. According to the agreement, 50,000 copies of each magazine may be sold. But Russians reported that copies of *Amerika* were hard to come by in Moscow, that newsstands ran out in no time, and that important people used all kinds of pull to get on the short subscription list. Having seen for myself that copies in the MGU library were dog-eared and crumbling from constant use, I was shocked to hear that Soviet authorities returned stacks of unsold copies to the American Embassy each month, saying that there was no demand for them. American officials speculated that the Soviet government limits sales of *Amerika* to match the meager sale of *Soviet Life* in the United States because it would be embarrassing to admit that Russians are more eager to read *Amerika* than Americans are to read *Soviet Life.* When I asked a Russian friend about the situation, he commented drily, "At least 20,000 copies of *Amerika* could be sold immediately at MGU."

Any American newspaper or magazine attracted immense curiosity. Lavishly illustrated, brightly made up magazines like *Life, Look, Saturday Evening Post,* or *Vogue* could draw a crowd in minutes. But I remember one young man in particular, a stealthy figure who stepped out of a shadow in the seventeenth-floor corridor at 1 A.M., blocked my way and whispered three words: *"New York Times."* He made them sound like some mysterious password. He continued to whisper, and I gathered that somehow he had learned that I subscribed to it. Obviously he was embarrassed to make a direct request, perhaps even afraid; yet he couldn't resist.

Dropping his voice even lower he murmured, "Can you lend me some copies?" His uneasiness was catching. I thought he was on the level, but I was not about to start passing out copies of *The Times* to a perfect stranger in a darkened corridor at one o'clock in the morning. I suggested that he drop by my room some other time for a chat. He never did.

Other Russians were just as curious to see *The Times* but they didn't waylay me in the hall to get it. They understood that I could not make it a practice to distribute the paper; after all, the Soviet government didn't ban its sale in Moscow so that American exchange students could take up the slack. But when students visited my room, they made a point of turning the pages of *The Times.* The very size and weight of the Sunday edition overwhelmed them, since *Pravda* and *Izvestia* are only four to eight pages. Those who could read English wondered where to begin; those who couldn't asked me to translate, then turned to the pictures. They were delighted with candid shots of world leaders, and especially Soviet leaders, because Soviet papers ordinarily print stiff and formal photos of dignitaries. They lingered with relish over occasional shots of Stalin and Khrushchev, whose portraits no longer appear in the Soviet press. And once when a Russian came across an old picture of Trotsky, there was a pause, a second look, and then a flash of recognition. "Ooh, Trotsky," he said, "So that's what you looked like."

My friends gazed sadly at photos of President Kennedy, and a number asked permission to cut them out. When I asked one why, he pointed to the portrait of JFK on the wall above my desk and observed shyly that he wanted one to put up in his room.

The color ads in *The Times Magazine,* with their testimony to American abundance, were magnets.

"Look at the oppressed American proletariat," joked a Russian.

"We should have it that bad," remarked his friend.

"Oy koshmar, kakoi koshmar—It's a nightmare," a *studentka* cried out in delight at the sight of mini-skirts, patterned mesh stockings, and brightly colored stretch pants.

Although Russians reacted to the affluence with almost uncritical enthusiasm, they sooner or later remembered to ask about poverty, crime in the streets, and racial discrimination. But the way they broached these *spornye voprosy*—controversial questions—was what impressed me. "Is it really true," they would ask, "that thirty million Americans live in poverty? Is it really true that New York is swarming with dope addicts and crime? Is it really true that white men who murder Negroes can go free in the South?"

Were they really uncertain or were they being polite? As time passed, I realized that they were intent on testing what they read in their own press against what an American would tell them. And they did not behave as if their side had scored when I acknowledged that thirty million Americans lived in poverty, that dope addiction was a serious problem in New York, and that white men who had murdered Negroes in the South had gone free. They seemed sympathetic when I said that we Americans were trying to alleviate and cure our national ills. Many even volunteered the opinion that the Soviet Union suffered from economic, social, and political maladies of its own. Instead of harping, as Soviet papers often do, on "the suppression of the American Communist Party," students asked what was wrong with a Party and doctrine that could attract only 10,000 American followers. At no time did anyone harangue me about historically inevitable crises of capitalism. And several times when I ventured to speak abstractly of capitalism and Communism, I was urged to talk instead of concrete problems.

Once an intense young economist from the U.S.S.R. Ministry of Finance, an MGU graduate, brought a list of written questions to a party.

"Skazhite pozhaluista (tell me, please)" he began. "What

do you think of Keynesian money policy?" But before I could say more than a few sentences he looked at his watch and, smiling apologetically, interrupted me.

"Skazhite pozhaluista—what do you think are the main differences between Soviet and American criminal law?"

Again I could make only a couple of points before he cut in to explain that this was the first time he had spoken at length to an American who knew Russian, and that's why he wanted to move on to the next question. So our conversation continued—a volley of *"skazhite pozhaluista's"* followed by questions: Who killed President Kennedy? What would President Kennedy have done differently in Vietnam had he lived? What would Barry Goldwater have done differently had he won? What was American policy toward social revolution in Latin America?

I never found out what he thought about any of these issues, and he certainly never paused long enough to find out what I did.

In the perspective of friendly exchanges, a few tense encounters stood out. A belligerent American-baiter cornered me at a party in the dorm and tried to prove that America was the aggressor in the Cuban missile crisis of 1962. He had no doubt about his facts, and to clinch his case, he trotted out his most devastating argument.

"Half the residents of Florida," he declared triumphantly, "were evacuated during the crisis in anticipation of an attack on Cuba."

The other Russians listening asked me if that were really so. I replied that to the best of my knowledge it was not. Then our host stepped in and cut off debate.

"New York is closer to Florida than Moscow is," he said to my adversary. "If that many people were evacuated, don't you think he would have heard about it in New York before we did in Moscow?"

Then there was the student who was reported to be passionately anti-American and itching to have at me. Mutual friends arranged a meeting and then sat in a circle around us to enjoy the confrontation. But my antagonist turned out to be a good-hearted fellow who couldn't bring himself to be contentious. He started to pose a stinger about American oil interests in Venezuela, then drew back.

"Do you mean to ask," I said, "why the ruling circles of the American monopolist bourgeoisie has imposed its reactionary imperialist yoke on the oppressed peoples of Latin America who are struggling to win their liberation?"

To hear an American, like a pompous announcer on Moscow Radio, intone the familiar charges in the familiar jargon was too much for my friends. Even my interrogator chuckled, and we spent the rest of the evening amicably.

Mocking old shibboleths, American as well as Soviet, was one way to disarm argumentative Russians. But my secret weapon, which was nearly always effective, was a determination to be honest about America even if that meant being critical. There are Americans who believe that no voice of America should criticize the U.S. in the U.S.S.R., that an American's job is to accentuate the positive. But my stay in Moscow convinced me that indiscriminate flag-waving does more harm than good.

What really impresses the Russians, far more than our affluence, is our right to criticize our government and social system openly and if need be furiously. What Soviet legislator would dare attack Brezhnev the way Fulbright laced into Johnson? What Soviet magazine would print pictures of Soviet police brutality as *Life* did of Alabama troopers in Selma? Are there American equivalents of Sinyavsky and Daniel who need to get their views published in other lands? Would Soviet students feel as free to criticize their system as I was to criticize mine?

"You know, you Americans are very clever," a Communist Party member said to me in a moment of candor. "Your best tactic is the way you maul one another in public. *Pravda,* of course, can't resist publishing the critical speeches of people like Fulbright. But those articles often backfire. Readers ask themselves why we don't have Fulbrights. Articles like that certainly don't paint a picture of a police state in America. In fact, the stupidest thing your Voice of America could do would be to suppress criticism. That's what our press used to do under Stalin, and some sections of it are still guilty. If you were to do that, people would no longer respect America."

My friend paused for a deep breath and then continued even more emphatically, "We should learn the technique from you. We have a lot of real debate at closed meetings. We should publicize more of it. Nobody really believes we are as unanimous as we sometimes pretend. We should be more open about our differences. Hell, all you have to do is drop in on a meeting of students with some Party lecturer. You'll hear plenty of fireworks, and on big issues, too."

The issue of Vietnam, I feared, would be the crucial test of my good relations with Russians, but it turned out to pose no obstacle. I noticed that Russians socialized very little with Vietnamese or Chinese. A remarkable number of Russians didn't want to talk about Vietnam at all. Some, perhaps, went out of their way to avoid embarrassing an American, but others, I felt sure, were apathetic.

"We're just tired of hearing about Vietnam," said one boy who was a Komsomol rank-and-filer. "There's been so much said and written that the truth will never be known. It's no use trying to fix the blame. If a bunch of fanatical Asians want to fight the strongest country in the world, and if you Americans want to get bogged down there, it's no business of ours. Let's just hope the war ends, and the sooner the better."

Other Russians, who wanted to talk about Vietnam, appeared to be surprisingly open-minded. When they asked me to explain the American point of view, I had the feeling that they were using me as a devil's advocate. There were steadfast opponents of American policy in Vietnam who didn't ask me about the American position—they knew what they were against—but even they conceded that North Vietnam had not been guiltless, that China's calls for wider conflagration were alarming, and that a great power like the United States could not always be expected to act like an angel.

But make no mistake about it. There were fiery supporters of North Vietnam who were impatient with their own government. They did not air their views directly to me. But I heard them complain at public meetings that big Soviet talk was not followed by enough action. They said they wanted their government to act more decisively to protect the North Vietnamese people from American bombs.

Irony piled upon irony. I thought of Americans raging at their leaders for allowing the war to continue. Here were Russians burning up because their government didn't take steps to inflame the conflict even further. Gingerly, I remarked on this to a Russian friend.

"Indeed it is ironic," he answered sadly. "The whole situation is ironic. What would you say if I told you that a lot of us are against American intervention in Vietnam not because of *Pravda,* but in spite of it? Our press has been so wrong so often that many young people read it skeptically. *Pravda* can run on for columns, and its exhortations convince few. But when it prints pictures of burned villages and maimed Vietnamese, it convinces a great many."

The extent of Russian interest in America was most vividly apparent at the meeting addressed by a *Pravda* correspondent. His description of his seven-year stint in the U.S. took place at a gathering charged with unusual excitement. The lounge was jammed and overheated, and after awhile the speaker became hoarse. But students would not allow him to leave. There was an air of objectivity about his talk of which they obviously approved. He was humorous at his own expense, as well as America's, and again this struck a responsive chord. They asked for an eyewitness account of Khrushchev banging his shoe on a table at the U.N., and then laughed as if it were a delicious comic routine. They wanted to know what representatives of other nations thought of Khrushchev's performance—clearly they were not proud of it. They asked how Americans treat Russians in the United States. The speaker replied that about one-third were warm and friendly, one-third polite but cool, and one-third were hostile. When someone asked about demonstrations in American streets, I expected him to bemoan the plight of "progressive Americans." Instead he replied, "You should see these Americans. They take to the streets to protest everything from the price of milk to the war in Vietnam. They march. They lie down and block traffic. They go inside and sit in and sleep in. It's really something."

Two speakers at a meeting on Britain drew a smaller, less excited gathering. Another Soviet correspondent was there to describe his years in London, as was a woman who had recently been there for a short stay. The correspondent spoke as frankly and gracefully as his colleague had talked about America, but the woman knocked everything—prices were too high, morals too low, music too loud, hair too long, skirts too short, workers too poor, bankers too rich, even noses too high in the air.

The audience reaction to her was sharp and bilingual.

"Kvatit," shouted someone in Russian.

"Enough," cried another in English.

"How do you know if you were only there for a few days?" yelled a third.

She glared at her audience and stormed out of the hall.

The correspondent, however, was asked to return, and the next time he brought slides of London and, by popular request, recordings of the Beatles. But for some reason the audience was cool to the sound of the big beat. The trouble, I learned later, was that he had recordings with which the students were familiar. What they had hoped for was something new. He realized that he was not getting the right kind of response and tried to explain. "You've really got to *see* the boys to appreciate them. I mean, they're really talented. Paul and John write a lot of the songs, and Ringo plays the drums. You really must see them."

Poor man! He had walked into a trap of his own making.

"When *will* we be able to see the Beatles? When will they be invited to the Soviet Union?"

The question came from one part of the hall and then was taken up by others like an echo. The speaker did not realize that rumors had recently been telling the university that the Beatles were indeed coming. There was even a story that they had arrived and were established in a Moscow hotel. Another yarn had it that they had stopped at Sheremyetevo Airport on their way to Japan and had given a performance on the Tarmac. Even a senior professor at the Juridical Faculty had told me in confidence that the Beatles had been invited for June. But a friend of mine pooh-poohed the whole thing.

"The professor must be out of his mind," he said. "Do you think Pavlov [Sergei Pavlov, the First Secretary of the Komsomol] wants those guys running around Moscow entertaining the New Soviet Man? Do you think Kosygin wants to spend scarce Soviet gold to import them?"

The correspondent, it turned out, didn't think the Beatles were coming either, and as far as I know they never did appear that year.

Next the correspondent showed his slides, which depicted London in a very attractive light. But his audience didn't come alive until he came to shots of Mme. Tussaud's Wax Works, with its figures of world leaders. Immediately a student had a question:

"Do they have any of our leaders there?"

"Yes."

"Do they have Bulganin there?" The loaded question tickled funny bones around the hall.

"No," replied the speaker with a straight face.

"Do they have Khrushchev there?" Louder laughter.

"They *did* have Khrushchev," said the correspondent, with only a trace of a grin. "But then they deposed him."

"Bravo!" The applause was for the correspondent's wit.

Meetings on Canada and Finland brought fine turnouts, and students stayed each time until the end. At the Canadian affair they watched with interest film shorts showing skiing in the Canadian Rockies and Canadian cowboys at a rodeo. The Finnish evening, a tribute to Sibelius on the anniversary of his birth, was devoted to his music, performed by Soviet musicians.

It was an entirely different story on International Student Day when the North Vietnamese and Poles shared the program. The Poles began with three film shorts and when they were over, half the Russians in the audience left. Most who remained were Vietnamese and Chinese. The first Vietnamese film was a documentary about a national hero, the youth who tried to assassinate Robert McNamara in Saigon but was caught and executed. The film was no more subtle than the North Vietnamese student in the hall who translated into Russian with a generous sprinkling of invective aimed at "the American enemy." It contrasted shots of American soldiers drinking and dancing in Saigon bars with pictures of mangled bodies of children, described as victims of American air raids.

More Russians left the hall after the first Vietnamese film. I was one of the few who remained for a full-length feature about a little boy who helps the Vietcong and is killed by American troops. Again the Vietnamese interpreter filled his commentary with scathing phrases about "the American enemy," until one of the last Russians in the hall cried out in exasperation, "Sit down. Let's see the film. Enough of this jabbering about the American enemy!"

15

Youth Talks Back

As I got to know my Soviet colleagues better, I noticed with increasing admiration their efforts to level with themselves and their society. I knew that they were continually asking questions and I was used to surprises. But even in my most optimistic moments I did not expect to hear anything as hair-raising as the following statement.

"Perhaps there should be more than one political party in the Soviet Union, not just the Communist Party. Perhaps there should be a party to represent farm workers; they haven't done too well in recent years. It's been said all these years that the Soviet state was a dictatorship of the proletariat. But didn't it really amount to a dictatorship of the Communist Party?"

These words were uttered, remember, in Moscow, not in New York, and not even by a Milovan Djilas in Belgrade. They were spoken by a Soviet student, and not privately, but at a public meeting in an MGU lounge where the speaker was no less than an official representative of the Moscow City Committee of the Communist Party.

I was not the only one in the room who was startled. Other Russians, students of law, economics, history, and philosophy, were also taken aback. After all, every Russian knows that Leninism *means* one-party rule. Since the Soviet people are supposed to be unanimous, they theoretically need only one party to express their political will. Under Stalin dissenters were jailed and executed for a lot less. Even today such opinions are never published. The statement created an uproar in the lounge; some students laughed nervously at their comrade's audacity; others could not suppress their reaction.

"Don't ask ridiculous questions. Don't be naïve," someone called out.

"What's wrong with the question? Every man has a right to speak," yelled another.

"Now the fun's beginning," exulted a third.

The man who provoked the storm chose to go no further. He sat down. And when no one else pressed the point the speaker decided to ignore it. In a sense he had an out—the evening's announced topic was "The International Situation." However, the audience would not allow him to stick to it.

"Was the cult of the personality accidental and unique in the Soviet Union, or is it a logical and inevitable stage in the development of all Communist states?"

The question was almost as unorthodox as the one before. The Party had pronounced its position on this as long ago as June, 1956; if the student didn't remember, the Party lecturer certainly did.

"The cult was not and is not a universal phenomenon," he said. "It was a product of the backwardness of our country, of our desperate need to industrialize and defend ourselves against capitalist encirclement, and, of course, of the aberrations of Stalin's own personality."

The questioner winked knowingly at his friends. "If that's the case," he said, "can you name a socialist country that has not had a cult of personality?"

The lecturer paused only for a moment. "Well, take the German Democratic Republic, for instance."

"What about Ulbricht?" the student shot back.

The student's friends applauded. The subject changed abruptly.

"Why do we always criticize the leader after he's gone?" came the next question from another part of the room. "Why did Brezhnev and Kosygin wait until Khrushchev was ousted before they denounced him? Let's suppose that Khrushchev had won and retained power. Wouldn't Brezhnev and Kosygin now be attacked as members of an anti-Party group headed by Suslov?"

"One can't answer such questions," said the lecturer with a smile. Several in the audience groaned.

"Why can't we read the works of Trotsky and Bukharin? It's impossible to get them in the library unless you have elaborate references. Some people think that is ridiculous."

With each new question I wondered just how far the students would go.

The speaker smiled benignly, almost superciliously. "Some people may want to read Trotsky and Bukharin, but, frankly, some couldn't care less. I'm simply not interested."

"Oh, come now," a student complained while others murmured skeptically. "To read Trotsky and Bukharin is not to become their disciples. They were important historical figures and we want to know more about them. That's all. We just want to know."

They wanted to know other things, too.

"Who leads the world in standard of living, the U.S.A. or Sweden?"

"Why don't you give out statistics comparing our standard of living with the capitalist countries?"

"Our economists tell us that there are no reliable criteria for comparing standards of living," answered the lecturer patiently. "A lot depends on different people's wants, customs, and climates."

I thought the speaker had a good point, but his listeners didn't.

"There *are* criteria for comparisons," someone objected.

"Just give us the statistics, and we'll give you the criteria," shouted another.

The meeting trailed off into less controversial subjects. On the dangerous developments in China speaker and students were in complete agreement. But the students had made their point. Like the man from the Central Committee, this Party lecturer had run into a barrage of tough and outspoken questions. He had kept his poise admirably. Nevertheless, I could only think that he returned to his Party colleagues with a disturbing report on the mood at MGU.

To study the mood and thinking of Soviet students, I sat in on a variety of MGU meetings on economic and political subjects attended by students from various faculties. Challenging questions from the floor were frequent, but the temper of each meeting varied with the subject and the speaker. Official Party representatives, professors of Party history, government officials, professors of economics, law, and mathematics—I was never sure in advance what to expect. Fireworks flared up where I least expected them. Or there might be none at all, which was also revealing.

Some meetings were organized by the faculties; others, by students. But all, in contrast to closed Party and Komsomol meetings, were open to the public and well advertised in advance. None was reported in the Soviet press, and of course there were no foreign reporters present. But no one was asked to identify himself or show his *propusk* at the door. None of the speakers knew me, but students in the audience who did acted as if I belonged. On occasion I even posed questions.

I rarely noticed other foreigners at the meetings. A few

American students attended one or two sessions; I went religiously to all. A British exchange scholar showed up regularly, but I gathered that he couldn't follow much of the discussion. After every meeting I transcribed notes into a diary I kept throughout the year.

A professor of economics came to the dormitory to discuss the Soviet economy in the light of the September, 1965, reforms, which, designed to increase the importance of profits, had been announced with tremendous fanfare by the Party Central Committee. I wondered whether there would be acrimonious debate.

The scholar's opening remarks, summing up the reforms, were brief and professional, and the audience listened quietly and attentively. Then, however, the chairman invited questions from the floor, the usual signal for excitement in meetings with Party lecturers.

"If our factories must make profits to survive under the new system, won't unprofitable enterprises have to close? And won't we have a lot of unemployment?"

Another student cut in before the speaker could reply: "Perhaps a little unemployment would be healthy. There are thousands doing useless jobs. We should pay them to stop working. Then we'd know how many productive jobs we have."

Another explosive session, I thought, with its interruptions, irreverences, and skepticism. But suddenly the storm subsided.

"We anticipate problems, of course," said the economist. "Some enterprises may have to close down, and workers will have to move. But the difference between us and the capitalists is that we are not after profits for profits' sake. We seek them only because they go with efficient production of the things people need. It wouldn't make sense to hurt the people whose welfare is our goal."

Did any Russians in the room think he was being a little

ingenuous about a system that has often put heavy industrial production ahead of consumption? Apparently not.

"We can't expect the reforms to solve all our problems overnight," the speaker continued. "We're supposed to be a planned economy, but we've often planned badly. For example, nobody studied the demand for sewing machines; they just produce them. Now we've got three billion rubles worth of unwanted sewing machines, and we've had to close three factories. We always studied the amount of metal to put in sewing machines. Now we've got to study what people want."

No one in the audience seemed astonished by the news. The listeners were like interns with a distinguished physician-teacher. Together they were calmly analyzing a fever chart.

"Speaking of planning," the economist went on, "did you ever hear about the mess in Byelorussia? They wanted to drill for oil, but the available appropriation was for a pipe line. So they laid a pipe line to bring in oil from a long way off. Then, suddenly, money became available for drilling. They drilled and struck oil. Now they don't need the pipe line, and the question is: What to do with it?"

"Use the line to pipe oil *out* of Byelorussia," suggested a student, sparking laughter from everyone.

"One of our big problems is sectionalism, isn't it?" someone asked.

"Yes, indeed. I'll give you an example. One of the provinces in Siberia has plenty of coal reserves and should have developed a nice mining industry. But no, they wanted a fancy and glamorous electronic industry. Now they have to haul in their coal from miles away."

"And what about *nauka upravleniia,* or business administration as the Americans call it?" put in another man. "Tereshchenko says we're way behind them in simple administrative efficiency."

Tereshchenko—I knew the name well for friends in Economics and Juridical Faculties were forever talking about him. He is a Soviet economist who spent many years in the United States, working in the Department of Agriculture and teaching business administration. Returning recently to live in the Soviet Union, he published a book, *Organization and Administration—U.S.A.*, which had become a bible for students and professors who prided themselves on being pragmatic and open-minded. At first I couldn't find a copy, for Tereshchenko's is one of these books—others are the works of popular poets—which sell out as soon as they go on sale. Of the 170,000 copies of the first two editions, I couldn't locate one. Even the library copies were always out. Finally a friend showed me his, which he had generously underlined, and I realized what the excitement was all about. Tereshchenko's book is essentially a plea that the U.S.S.R. learn some important lessons of administrative efficiency from the U.S.A. He allots only a few paragraphs to what he thinks is wrong with American capitalism and devotes the body of the book to what is right and sensible. I was surprised that Tereshchenko took time to discuss trivial methods of saving labor and money such as permitting workers to use company phones on company time to avoid wasteful trips to phone booths and encouraging use of such items as Scotch tape instead of messy Soviet paste, ball point pens instead of messy Soviet fountain pens, and pencil sharpeners instead of pocketknives. But he goes on to make some major recommendations. He condemns the widespread practice of "storming" to fulfill plans ahead of schedule on the grounds that it is wasteful; American experience shows, he says, that bursts of concentrated labor are followed by long unproductive periods. He suggests that Saturday morning shifts are not sufficiently profitable because, as American studies show, workers need time to swing into a good rhythm and because heat is wasted when the plant closes down early. Most striking of all, he ridicules the old Communist obsession with cutting down white collar administrative staffs.

"Of course Tereshchenko's right," said the professor of economics. "We must get out of the habit of cutting down staffs simply for the sake of cutting them. We fire several secretaries, and what happens? The engineer we pay to make decisions ends up typing his letters himself. Does that make economic sense? For too long we've idolized the worker at the bench, the big bear. We should remember that bears spend half their time hibernating."

"Perhaps we should recruit experts from American business schools to help us," suggested a student. "After all, we hired American engineers during the thirties to help build our dams."

"Well, I'm not sure about American business schools," returned the economist with a grin. "But we must be ready to learn from the West. We should send more people abroad to study. There is no Communist way to run a factory any more than there is a Communist way of putting a car together. You all know that we're buying a huge auto assembly plant from Fiat, don't you? Well, at one point someone on top decided to save money by not buying the computer system that's part of the plant. They asked us to work out our own computer system here at the university. Well, we hit the roof. We refused. If we're going to learn from the Italians, let's get the whole complex and study it."

As cozy as an unruffled seminar in an American university, the meeting was the calmest I attended at MGU—for there was agreement even on criticism. The professor, who was more than likely a Party member but not a hired Party hand, had come to speak as an expert on economics, not to lay down the Party line. How would he have reacted if the students had harried him with hot ideological questions? The point was that they did not. Another session involving a professor and students of economics was relatively tranquil as long as they hewed to their subject. But when they veered off on a political tangent the meeting became livelier. The professor was a Party figure of some consequence. Finding a seat in the lounge, I wondered how the students would treat an academic expert who was also an official representative of the establishment.

The smartly attired speaker, who was also a deputy to a borough council, had the look and easy grace of a Kennedy. He remarked casually that he swam an hour a day in the university pool, and during the meeting he paced back and forth with arms folded across his chest, then sat down at a table and put his feet up. Almost at once the session turned into a dialogue between him and Misha, a burly disheveled student wearing sandals without socks, floppy blue sweat pants with shirt tail hanging out, and thick glasses. Each time Misha asked a question, he surfaced from his easy chair, lumbered a few feet to the speaker's table, flicked his cigarette over the ashtray, and then subsided again into his chair.

The deputy surveyed some recent accomplishments in his district: 160,000 square meters of roads built or repaired, 40,000 trees planted. But housing was "the question of questions," and he predicted it would take six more years to build suitable homes for people who still lived in rickety houses, tiny rooms, and dank cellars.

"But Ivan Alekseevich!" It was Misha on his feet, flicking ashes. "Aren't you forgetting the important people who use pull to get more space than they need without waiting in line like everybody else?"

Misha's friends nodded their agreement. "Yes," Ivan Alekseevich replied. "I shouldn't have passed over that point. Take the case of husband and wife living in one room with an adolescent son. That's not healthy. But on the other hand, the Rector of MGU keeps several good apartments with which to attract faculty members. That's life. You know and I know that matters would be even worse if we didn't have a passport system to keep people out of Moscow who have no apartment here."

"But Ivan Alekseevich!" Misha was again on his way to the ashtray. "That passport system is stupid and arbitrary. There must be a more democratic way."

Again students nodded agreement with Misha, but the mood was still amiable. It was Ivan Alekseevich himself who led the meeting into controversy. "Well, *rebiata,* what do you think? What's the state of Marxism-Leninism today? I'm against revisionism, of course. But a hundred years is a long time. There have been a lot of changes in the world since Marx thought it all up."

"Ivan Alekseevich!" Misha was on his feet again. "Let's not be naïve. How can anyone expect an American worker who earns one hundred to two hundred dollars a week to revolt? If you show him the Soviet Union he'll just laugh. Nowadays the bourgeois liberals are saying that the decline in capitalism is moral. And we ourselves may run into a little moral decay when we get rich. Of course there will still be social revolutions in Asia, Africa, and Latin America—that's probably inevitable. But do we really want those people for allies?"

Ivan Alekseevich looked as if he thought Misha had gone too far, but before he could reply another student spoke up. "What's the latest on war, Ivan Alekseevich, is it inevitable or not?"

"War is not inevitable. But sometimes I think that we demobilize our people psychologically when we keep saying that. What we really need in this country is more preparedness."

"Ivan Alekseevich!" Again Misha. "How can you say that? As it is, we are warned too much to be vigilant."

"Listen, Misha, I'm not a dogmatist. I just think we've got to be ready. We've got to remember the Chinese, too. Mao and his group are stirring up real hatred in China, turning

700,000,000 people against us. They're fanatics. Did you hear about the man who took his wife's only blanket to stop a leak in a dike? Do you know they teach children to shout curses across the border at us?"

There was angry grumbling in the lounge. But as good old Misha, emerging from his chair, walked stolidly to the ash-tray, the buzzing ceased.

"Ivan Sergeevich," he began absent-mindedly.

"Ivan Alekseevich is the name," the professor corrected him.

"Ivan Alekseevich." Misha was unperturbed. "I think you make a mistake if you don't distinguish carefully between China's leaders and the Chinese people, and I'm afraid many of us are beginning to forget that distinction. We once had real affection for the Chinese, and that was a good thing. Brotherhood is a good thing, Ivan Alekseevich, and I'm afraid we may be losing it. It's not the fault of our leaders or press—they've been quite restrained. I just hope they never start to play on feelings of distrust for yellow people, because that could get out of hand."

I went with special anticipation to a session devoted to briefing students on the recently ended Twenty-third Communist Party Congress. At the Congress, the first since 1961, the Party had summed up the past four years, analyzed the present state of the Soviet Union, and agreed on Directives for the next Five-Year Plan. The proceedings had been hailed in the press and on radio and television as a triumph. At MGU, the speakers were an economist from Gosplan, the high and mighty State Planning Commission, which prepares the nation's economic plan; a professor of law; and a professor of Party history. Many Russians had made clear to me their contempt for Party history as an academic subject. I suspected that if the meeting got stormy the Party historian might draw lightning.

The man from Gosplan was frank and self-critical:

"Gosplan set the goals of the last Seven-Year Plan too high. This time *tovarishch* Kosygin told us to set them lower and more realistically so that we'll be able to beat them. That's what we did, and that's what we'll do."

"You admit that Gosplan was way off in its prediction for the Seven-Year Plan," said a student calmly and analytically. "But how is that possible? You're supposed to be scientific, aren't you? If not, you might as well close up shop."

"Our predictions in 1959 were all right," the economist defended himself. "The real villain was the weather, which crippled agriculture, thus slowing down whole branches of industry."

"But isn't there any way to end these impossible promises?" The young man posing the question seemed genuinely distressed. "We aren't criticizing Gosplan for the fun of it. It's just that this has happened so many times before. You promise. You fail. And then you promise to be more realistic next time. Why should anyone believe you this time?"

"Khrushchev kept pressing us to raise the targets in 1959," said the man from Gosplan self-righteously. "He told us that the economy would surely grow at a rapid pace."

As ripples of laughter spread across the room, the economist announced that he had to leave—rather abruptly, I thought. Next, the professor of Party history invited questions. I thought the Party historian looked more like a farmer than an academic: his shabby brown suit hung loosely on his sturdy frame, his four or five hairs were pasted in parallel lines across his pate, and he stood awkwardly, as if uncertain where to put his big red hands. I was about to kick myself for judging a man by external appearances when he explained that he had been a collective-farm chairman before turning to Party history.

Immediately I sensed a change of mood. Students had challenged the Gosplan economist, but their tone had been serious. Now the first question was positively playful.

"What's the latest word on Khrushchev's old slogan that 'this generation will live under Communism'? Will we still make it by 1980?"

The Party historian pondered the question earnestly. "As far as I am aware, that particular line is still in effect. I don't believe any doubts were expressed on that subject at the Party Congress."

"Why were no doubts expressed at the Congress?" came the inevitable question from the floor. "After all, the slogan is clearly open to doubt. Why was there no debate at all at the Congress? Why can't there be the kind of debate there was at the Tenth Party Congress in 1921?"

"You can't expect today the kind of debate they had at the Tenth Congress," the professor replied. "In those days there was real opposition. Today we are united."

"All right," the questioner pressed ahead. "Let's take the Fifteenth Congress in 1927. Then everyone was in agreement when they attacked Kamenev. But they still disagreed about other things."

"There is no need to cite the Fifteenth Congress," said the Party historian stubbornly. "That was forty years ago."

"Well, all I can say," said the student, "is that even the Twenty-second Congress seemed wider and more interesting than this one."

The questioner sank back in his seat resigned to a stalemate, but the Party expert could not resist one last thrust. "The Twenty-third Congress has been hailed throughout the world as serious and businesslike, so I don't know why you object. But I'll say this: I think we can expect some controversy at the coming *Inter-Kolkhoz* Congress."

"Who cares about the Inter-Collective Farm Congress?" someone shouted. "That's small change."

A student sitting on the window sill, whom I knew to be a member of the Party, recalled that Khrushchev had split the Party into two industrial and agricultural branches in 1962, and Brezhnev and Kosygin had reunited it after Khrushchev was deposed in 1964. "Why didn't anyone object when Khrushchev made the original mistake?" he asked. "Podgorny himself led the cheers for Khrushchev."

"Wait a minute," objected the Party historian. "People did object. Right here in MGU the Party History *Kafedra* of the Natural Sciences Faculties was against Khrushchev's reform, while in the Humanities Faculties the Party History *Kafedra* was for it. Those who supported Khrushchev were wrong, but they were sincerely wrong."

"Oh, great," cried someone sarcastically. "It's comforting to know they were sincere."

The Party historian turned to the student who had raised the subject. "You should know better than to ask questions like that," he said reproachfully. "You're a Communist yourself."

When the noise died down, the speaker took another tack. He tried being expansive, as if that were the way to control the meeting. "You know, *rebiata,* the Central Committee of our Party received more than a hundred thousand letters before the Congress, some containing questions like the ones you've been asking tonight. Why, they even got a letter from *tovarishch* Molotov."

"What did he have to say?"

"Yes, tell us."

"But don't reveal any state secrets, Nikolai Ivanovich."

"Oh, don't worry," Nikolai Ivanovich assured them. "I won't."

"Why did the Congress drop the title of First Secretary of the Party and adopt Stalin's old title of General Secretary instead? Do they want to go back to the cult of personality?"

The Party historian appeared shocked by the question. "There can be no return to the cult of personality," he said. "Our Party has made its position clear on that. The title of General Secretary is a Leninist title. A party may have a First

Secretary or a General Secretary or a Chairman. These are only titles."

The third speaker, the law professor, took over. Discussing provisions of a proposed new constitution, he mentioned the possibility of choosing officials for government bureaus by popular vote rather than by appointment.

"In the Ministry of Education," he said.

"Let us know when we can elect the Minister," someone shouted, triggering laughter.

"No," the jurist continued. "It's the school principals who may be elected."

"By whom?"

The ironic answer came from a student: "By the local Party Committee." Another burst of laughter.

"Why do our policemen have to carry billy clubs if we live under socialism?"

"Many of you are law students," the law professor retorted. "You should know how badly we need them."

The Party Congress was the subject of another meeting, this one attended mostly by students from the Mathematics Faculty and addressed by a professor of mathematics as well as academic experts on Party affairs. How did *matematiki* (mathematicians)—acknowledged to be the elite of the university—react to the Congress? When I arrived a student was praising the Party for not rehabilitating Stalin. But then he complained that important Congress speakers had attacked writers like Solzhenitsin who told the truth about Stalin's prison camps. "Writers must be free," he said, "free to depict mistakes made in the past."

An elderly wizened expert on Party affairs rose to reply. Setting his feet firmly apart, he hooked his thumbs into his belt, took a deep breath, and began:

"The trouble in our country today is that young people like you and these so-called writers whom you defend are manifesting a dangerous one-sidedness. You recall only the bad things that happened in the past. You know only how to criticize and tell us what's wrong. This is not a correct Party approach. Instead of fostering Communist consciousness in the masses, these writers propagate pessimism, skepticism, and decadence. This cannot be tolerated. The youth of today . . ."

The youth of today could not tolerate him.

"What do you know about youth? What right do you have to condemn us?"

"You're the one who's guilty of one-sidedness."

"Where have you been for the last thirty years? Have you forgotten what happened after the war?"

The outburst was so violent that the little man chose the better part of valor and sat down. A young woman, also an expert on Party affairs, replaced him. Choosing her words carefully, she conceded the need to keep in mind "Stalin's mistakes" as well as his achievements. "But there is no excusing a writer like Solzhenitsin who seems to have forgotten entirely about our accomplishments."

"What's wrong with Solzhenitsin?"

"What makes you an expert on literature?"

She lashed back. "You young people are impossible." She looked no older than they. "You seem to have some kind of fixation about Solzhenitsin and these other writers."

A third specialist on the Party, a man of about forty, spoke up: "Let's be sensible. Nobody's asking you to forget the cult. We only suggest that you don't become obsessed with it. Why don't we spend some time celebrating our victory in the Second World War? Let's build monuments to that. There are just too many books carping on past mistakes."

"What do you mean by too many books?"

"I once sat down and read them, and I could name ten right now."

"*Davaite*—let's hear them."

The speaker named three, then threw up his hands. "I give

up," he said, laughing, and immediately the hostility diminished.

"If you're interested," spoke up a student, "I'll tell you why we must always remember the mistakes of the past. Because otherwise the same things could happen again. We recognize that many great things were accomplished and they deserve praise. But there are plenty of writers who praise them. Why do you attack the few critical writers? Why don't you complain about all the novels filled with *poshlost'* (banality) ? Why did speakers at the Congress attack *Novy Mir?* Why didn't they let Tvardovsky speak at the Congress?"

The students turned to the professor of mathematics, a distinguished looking man of about sixty, for comment.

"I agree with you in part," he said. "I didn't admire all the speeches at the Congress, and in particular I didn't like *tovarishch* Sholokhov's tone. Neither do I agree with the speakers tonight who attach Solzhenitsin." He glanced with a touch of disdain at his fellow panelists. "He is a fine writer and should be encouraged. I know of no Party directive that forbids him or anyone else from writing critically about the past. But others have the same freedom to write more positively, and we need that, too. If you want monuments I can suggest the example of the Latvian writer whose father was executed. He collected his father's papers and published them. Recently they were translated into Russian and printed in Moscow."

The students did not interrupt the mathematician. Clearly they respected him. Yet I thought they seemed disappointed that he had not supported them more warmly. Instead, he had provided a third, mediating point of view. But no one, it occurred to me, had expressed a fourth opinion, that the creative artist should have no obligation except to tell his own truth in his own way.

The moment came when the mathematician stepped on the brakes. On such matters as the rights of writers and evaluations of the past he had been almost at one with the students. But when the issue was lack of dissent at the Twenty-third Congress, he parted company with them.

"You can't create dissent where it doesn't exist," he said, choosing to ignore the fact that it existed in that very room. "The delegates to the Congress were in agreement. For people who didn't read the whole transcript, you are awfully glib with your conclusions."

In short, in a showdown, the respected mathematician stood with the Party hack.

16

Dissent in Perspective

How deep was student dissatisfaction? Did their comments and behavior at meetings truly reflect their views and mood? Months of private conversations helped to give me perspective. Once I asked a Russian point blank what the turbulent meetings meant.

"The students who talk back to Party speakers are not rebellious," said my friend, who had done a little talking back in his time. "They're just restless. They mean what they say when they criticize, but sometimes they get carried away. Remember that a Party official represents the official view. Sometimes they want to see how far they can push him. When the speaker is flexible, they feel they're winning. When the speaker is a *starik* (old man) who can only tell you what he learned in the thirties, then it's too bad, but it can also be entertaining."

Judged by this standard, some of the most entertaining *stariki* at MGU were likely to be found teaching Party history and scientific Communism. For example, there was the elderly Party historian who worked himself up to such an ideological frenzy that he ended a lecture shouting: "Long live the Communist Party of the Soviet Union. Long live toilers of the U.S.S.R."

"The fellows in class stood and cheered the old man," a witness to the event told me. "He was so overwhelmed he didn't realize we were laughing at him."

Or the professor of Party history who in 1963 solicited contributions from his class to send Khrushchev a congratulatory birthday telegram.

"Everybody thought he was a little touched," recalled one of his students, "but we humored him and even inflated the praise a little to give Nikita Sergeevich a thrill."

What happened when elderly professors of this breed became angry with their irreverent charges? Once a student told a Party historian that "collectivization of Soviet agriculture only succeeded in making all the peasants equally poor."

"Who was your grandfather, young man?" the old man inquired threateningly. "Was he a *kulak* or a landowner?"

The wrong answer to a question like that could send men to Siberia in the thirties. But not in 1966. "The fellows in class couldn't stop laughing," I was told. "Someone yelled 'Get the *kulak* swine,' and that just made everyone laugh harder."

How many professors of Party history evoked this kind of reaction? What percentage of MGU students barely tolerated their required courses on Party history and scientific Communism? I don't know. I did meet students specializing in Party history who were as emancipated as their peers in less political fields. But an awful lot of Russians winked, giggled, or shrugged when I asked about these subjects, and many didn't hesitate to describe them as a waste of time. Some friends jokingly quizzed me to see how much Party history and scientific Communism I had learned at Harvard and Columbia. One girl, a mathematician, asked me to explain some "doctrines of anti-Communism," since she expected a question on that subject on an exam. I outlined for her the most telling American criticisms of Communism that I could think of and she carefully noted them down. Later she reported gleefully that she had quoted these remarks, identifying an American as her source, and had received the top grade of five. No hack, that professor.

Is Communist ideology losing its appeal? I met no one at MGU who was losing sleep worrying over the world revolution, the coming of "full Communism," or the withering away of the state. No one expected the workers of the world to unite. The Western proletariat, they knew, had a lot more to lose than its chains. Notwithstanding the Party's pledge, young Russians did not expect to "live under Communism," and they expressed grave doubts about the viability of a system "based on the principle of 'from each according to their abilities to each according to his needs.' " Men will always disagree about what they need, I was told. Some students refused to discuss the distant future on the grounds that it was irrelevant. And when we talked about my research topic, community participation in Soviet city affairs, they warned me not to interpret this as a step toward the withering away of the state, which is exactly how some official Soviet spokesmen liked to interpret it.

Yet almost every student I met at MGU praised Soviet progress, which they spelled out as the new industrial might, the achievements in space, free education and medical care, low-cost housing and transportation. They attributed that progress to the country's socialist system. The very students who talked back to Party speakers told me that no one could criticize the Soviet Union without understanding its past.

I remember one man in particular, not a Party member or Komsomol activist, who brought up the subject as we sat drinking tea at three o'clock one winter morning. He was all wound up, tired but intense. The speech he delivered was as much for his own benefit, I thought, as for mine.

"The Revolution took place when Russia was poor and

wounded by war, and we've lived through some terrible times since then. I'm not looking for pity, and I'm not justifying everything that was done. I'm not blaming all our troubles on the capitalist encirclement, though you didn't help. All I'm saying is that we began with a huge mass of illiterate impoverished peasants, lived through a world war, Civil War, and world war again, lost more than twenty million people, not to mention economic wealth, to Hitler, and yet look what we've managed to build. Do you think we like to stand in all these long lines and endure these shortages? Of course not. But we understand why they exist.

"I'm not saying that our system is perfect, far from it. But capitalism and Western socialism would have been impossible under Russian conditions. We needed a tough kind of socialism, including total economic planning and even use of force. Yes, innocent people were killed. But how many innocent people starved in the famines before 1917, and how many innocent soldiers were butchered fighting for the Tsar? Perhaps the difference is that Stalin and his associates planned and ordered their killings while people died quietly before 1917 and thought some kind of impersonal fate was responsible. But the system itself was responsible before 1917 and Stalin, for all his crimes, was building a better system.

"Today many of us are impatient. We want to move ahead faster. But we're trapped by our past. Old habits are still strong. People in important places are afraid of change. But our leaders are not evil men. They aren't accumulating power for its own sake. Some may be hidebound. Others are too cautious. And some are simply stupid. But they're trying sincerely to build the country."

Not every student I knew would have agreed with every word of this passionate discourse. But many would have agreed with most of it. For them, as for the majority, I would guess, neither capitalism nor Western socialism was a realistic alternative to Soviet Communism. What they wanted was a more humane, more democratic, more efficient Communism, which would live up to its own promises, obey its own strictures, and abide by its own constitution.

Take the Party itself. As far as I could tell, the student who spoke in favor of another political party was very much in the minority.

"Most of us are more realistic," another friend confided during a quiet talk in his *blok*. "What we really want is to have the Party operate better. We have some fine Party rules, you know, democratic centralism and all that. There's supposed to be unlimited debate until a decision is taken and then strict discipline. That's the way it was before Lenin died and later in the twenties. Why can't it be that way again? The Party Rules call for criticism and self-criticism. That's what we need."

Or take Soviet elections. The official Soviet justification for the one man, one vote, one candidate system is that the Soviet people are one. But the students I saw casting their ballots to the tune of patriotic music on the loudspeaker were only bored. When I asked a friend whom he meant to vote for, he asked me whom I would recommend.

"You're the only one I know who reads all the election speeches in *Pravda*," he said with a mischievous grin. "Tell me who looks good this year."

Another friend, standing beside me as we studied a campaign poster extolling the virtues of a none-too-dark horse named Aleksei Nikolaevich Kosygin, said, "It's bad enough to say we're choosing when we have no choice. But we make it worse by saying that ours are the most democratic elections in the world."

If not another political party, what was the alternative?

"We could simply have several candidates for each post," said a law student who had obviously been thinking about the problem. "The Constitution doesn't forbid that. On the contrary, Article 141 says nominations may be made by groups like trade unions and cooperatives. Let all candidates be acceptable to the Party. Let them differ only on small things and in education and experience. At least that would be a start."

We heard at MGU that the Commission working on the new constitution had been considering just such an alternative.

"They realize all too well how debilitating the present system is," said someone close to the Commission. "They know that intellectuals laugh at it. But they can't agree what to do about it. The voters aren't used to choices like that."

"Of course they have to be cautious," said a skeptic. "What do you think the masses would do if you put a candidate in opposition to Brezhnev? They'd vote against Brezhnev, that's what they'd do. Not because they're against him, but just to see what would happen. You must remember that there are a lot of simple people in this country who never had a choice before. They tinker with anything new to see how it works. Just look at them at airports, on subways. They're still trying to figure it all out. Let's be realistic. The elections bother the intellectuals. *Nichevo*. What do intellectuals count for even in your country? As long as the masses are satisfied, everything's all right. In ten years the masses will be more sophisticated and demanding and they'll have more cars and washing machines to keep them happy. That will be the time to make a change."

"Let's be realistic." Any number of Russians would begin with this phrase and invariably it was a prelude to cynicism. In the beginning I was surprised because so many seemed to be inquiring spirits, ardent seekers after truth. But the honesty that demolished cant made them realists.

Surely there could be no more crucial test than the case of Sinyavsky and Daniel. There was a protest meeting at the Philological Faculty and those who took part, I heard through the not always reliable grapevine, were severely disciplined. But these brave ones were the exceptions. At the meetings I attended I heard no one speak out against the trial and very few wanted to discuss the subject in private. I was assured by several friends, however, that hardly anyone at MGU approved of the verdict.

"The great majority of the intelligentsia," said a graduate student in law, "think that the trial was unfair. They think that the issue was moral and not criminal. Most of us think that Sinyavsky and Daniel were wrong to send their work abroad, to say one thing at home and the opposite abroad. They should have done their criticizing at home. But the government was wrong to make such a fuss. All it did was draw attention to the books, and we lost a lot of respect in the West."

But how could Sinyavsky and Daniel have done their criticizing at home? Surely the authorities never would have published their work. My friend obviously had that on his mind, too. "No," he said, "the books wouldn't have been published. But you must remember that we have no tradition of absolute freedom for the writer. It's hard to argue that he can publish whatever he wants or that the state should subsidize something that slanders the state. Furthermore you must keep in mind the mass of readers. Perhaps it's too soon to give them works that attack our system. The cultural question is the toughest problem we have. The leaders want to encourage writers but fear that they will go too far. Twenty years ago Sinyavsky and Daniel would have been executed. Today, they only get a few years. Ten years from now their works will be published. Isn't that progress?"

At their trial the writers denied that they had meant to slander the Soviet State and people and rejected the prosecution's attempt to equate their opinions with those of the most negative characters in their books. My friends had no way of evaluating these arguments because they had no access to the offending works. But everyone was confident that underground copies would soon be circulating in Moscow.

In all their questioning, students rarely complained about specific Party leaders by name. They were not interested in personalities or relative power position in the Kremlin. Did members of the Politburo differ in their policies? How had they combined to defeat Khrushchev? Were they competing again for power, and if so who stood for what, and who would win? If Russians pondered these questions they never admitted it to me. When Mikoyan stepped down as Soviet President and the edition of *Izvestia* that carried the news was delayed, I was more excited than my Soviet friends, who assured me that the change meant nothing. When Podgorny was announced as Mikoyan's successor, a couple of students from the Ukraine teased their Russian colleagues that a Ukrainian had replaced an Armenian as the head of state, and the Russians grumbled good-naturedly that this was a disgrace. But no one took the matter seriously. When my friends heard I was reading all the speeches at the Party Congress to see if there were any subtle differences in content and tone, they told me not to waste my time. Any real debate at the Congress was as likely, one said, "as a collision between the earth and a couple of stars." They were right, and they took pleasure in telling me so. Several even took the trouble to analyze all the speeches and then, like prospectors who had found gold, they demonstrated that nearly every address followed the same pattern and made the same six points. Every speaker 1) praised the Congress' businesslike character; 2) celebrated national achievements; 3) celebrated local triumphs in his bailiwick; 4) lamented a few scattered mistakes; 5) blasted America on Vietnam and 6) "Long live'd" the Communist Party of the Soviet Union.

It often seemed to me that departed Soviet leaders interested my friends more than present ones. Any mention of Stalin commanded attention, his picture drew stares, a walk past his grave in front of the Kremlin wall produced hushed silence, and, as some said, the way a man talked about Stalin was a good touchstone for telling how he might view the rest of the world. If some Party speakers told students to concentrate on the good done by Stalin, most students I knew would have agreed with Yevtushenko in his poem "Stalin's Heirs":

> And I appeal to our government,
>   with a request:
> to double,
>   and triple,
>   the guard at the grave,
> so that Stalin cannot rise again
>   and, with Stalin,
>   the past.

The names of Stalin's close associates, Molotov, Malenkov, and Kaganovich, did not evoke the same awe. These men had been defeated by Khrushchev; therefore, they were human. I knew several students who were "Molotov-watchers." Apparently the old man continued to live in the neighborhood of Lenin Library in a luxurious building that also housed other Soviet dignitaries, and it was his habit to take an afternoon constitutional. I saw him myself several times in Lenin Library. He was instantly recognizable to anyone who remembered his pictures in the press. He still wore the rimless glasses; he was still ramrod straight. Invariably he was occupied with what looked like a manuscript—his memoirs? If I'd had the cheek I would have approached and looked.

There was a story going the rounds that one day a Russian student did approach. "Good morning, *tovarishch* Molotov," he said, and the old man replied, "Good day, young man, but my name is Scriabin." That was Molotov's pre-Bolshevik name, and that was the entire conversation. What was its purpose? For the young Russian it was merely a chance to exchange a word with a once awesome personage.

My friends reserved for Khrushchev a special affection and special disdain. They laughed as they recalled his crudities of speech and behavior, but they were also ashamed that a boor had been their country's leader. What had we in the West thought of him? they asked, obviously fearing that we had thought the worst. When I said some Americans had enjoyed his earthy approach, they confessed that they had, too. Russians who dropped by my room never failed to chuckle at a *New York Times* picture of the corpulent Khrushchev greeting the tall elegant Kennedy at Vienna. How they would have prized a photograph of the former First Secretary banging that shoe at the U.N. or throwing that tantrum because he couldn't go to Disneyland! Everybody seemed to have a Khrushchev story. We happened to be looking at a picture of him chatting with some Soviet workers, and a Russian friend was reminded of the time a miner asked Khrushchev for a seven-hour day and Nikita Sergeevich replied, "You already have a seven-hour day. You work for seven hours and for one hour you tell jokes about me."

In a serious moment my friend summed up what he thought Khrushchev's real contribution had been. "He destroyed two important myths. By revealing Stalin's crimes, he cracked people's faith in the past. That had to be done to clear the air, rectify many wrongs, and prevent them from happening again. But he also shattered people's faith in an overoptimistic future. His pledge that we would overtake America by 1970 and his promise that this generation will live under Communism were as destructive as they were bombastic."

If young Russians laughed at Khrushchev, they laughed at themselves, too, and in the process confounded the Party's efforts to cast them as selfless worker-heroes. Many of my friends had spent a summer working as unskilled construction laborers in the Virgin Lands of Kazakhstan. They had volunteered to serve Party, Komsomol, and country and had been hailed by all three. But even as they performed this service they preserved an ironic sense of their own limitations.

"In the beginning of the summer we had fun," recalled a slight girl, a chemistry *studentka* who scarcely looked strong enough to make the trip. "We were packed like sardines in the train on the long trip out and when we got there we worked all day, sat around a campfire at night, and slept in tents. The first month was a lark. But the second month was a bore and by the end of the third we could have slit our throats."

"It's tough work, all right," said one of the boys who had volunteered to return for a second summer. "But the pay is fantastic. When we get out there we'll work overtime, overfulfill the plan, and make a lot of money. If the pay were poor we might not go back, but that doesn't mean we're cynical money grubbers or some kind of new bourgeoisie. We believe in building up our country, but we don't want to do it for nothing. This way we help the country and help ourselves, too."

"In the old days all the kids went gladly," another student told me. "But now a lot of freshmen are saying that they don't want to go. They say that kind of contribution should not be obligatory under socialism. They say that if it's really voluntary, then some will go and others will not."

"The truth is that a lot of kids are tired of *bor'ba* (the struggle)," I was told by a girl who had worked in Kazakhstan. "They admire the way their fathers struggled in the past, and they're ready to work hard at their own specialties. But they don't think it makes sense to send a physicist to lay bricks. They're tired of politics if it means empty speeches and crusades. Perhaps this mood is healthy; maybe it's unfortunate. But the fact is, it exists."

Since the Communist Party strongly encourages political activism, the man who chooses to be apolitical is not high in its esteem. But the time has passed when to be apolitical is a grave, perhaps insurmountable, handicap. Nevertheless, rejection of politics implies a basic criticism. The most disenchanted at MGU were not necessarily those who talked back to Party speakers but those who would not discuss Party doctrine and seduously avoided any taint of active involvement. If others wanted to be activists in the Komsomol and join the Party, that was their business. These "internal émigrés," as they were scathingly called by Komsomol leaders, retreated deep into their private lives. In the evenings they gathered with like-minded friends behind closed doors and spent the night and early morning talking, singing, and dreaming about anything but ideology.

Were these young men and women completely alienated? From bombast and cant, emphatically. They did not joke about speeches at the Party Congress, considering them beneath contempt. The sight of me reading those speeches in *Pravda* did not amuse them, as it did my more activist friends, but seemed actually to offend them. The very fact that I had chosen to spend a year at MGU puzzled them. Why should anyone who could be in America elect a year in the Soviet Union?

Their alienation did not assume exhibitionistic forms. They did not affect outlandish costumes or take to growing unkempt beards; where the establishment does not make a fetish of high style there is no need to rebel by being sloppy or dirty. I never heard of anyone taking drugs. I did know several who sometimes went on a binge of vodka when they received their monthly stipends. They did not mope or loaf or indulge in excesses of self-pity, and they did not drop out of school. On the contrary, they worked hard in the courses that interested them. They were not alienated by the impersonality of their vast Soviet multiversity. They prized the bigness of MGU. What they were against was the smallness of its political and ideological vision. They were, in effect, the Soviet Union's private men and women.

How large is this group at MGU? Of course no one can tell for certain, but I would guess they are a fairly small minority. I ran into more than a score of them, and I guessed there were many more, but they were not easy to get to know. Because they prized their privacy, they would not communicate their deepest convictions to a foreigner. Although strongly attracted to America, they made no special effort to cultivate an American's friendship. They were too proud and self-reliant.

The majority of the people I met belonged somewhere in the middle, between the dedicated activists and the internal émigrés. One man might join the Party despite his doubts and another might hold back because of them. The line between the two was not nearly so wide as one would think.

A fairly active *komsomolets* told me that he did not intend to join the Party. Being a Party member would speed his career, he explained. But he could not bear the thought of ever serving as a Party speaker. He did not want to twist and turn and, in the name of Party discipline, say what he did not believe.

"It's a difficult decision to stay out of the Party when you have ideals," he said dispassionately. "Because the power is in the Party, and that's the place where you can have real influence. There are a lot of fine people in the Party who are trying to improve things. It's easy to say that the worst people in the Party are careerists and the best are opportunists. What is an opportunist? Some are good people who keep compromising in the hope that someday they'll get the chance to do the great deed that justifies all the retreats. Who's to say they're wrong or less courageous than the man who stays outside, giving up his chance to have real influence? I stay out because that's my nature, but I don't condemn others for going in. You've probably got the same thing in America. There must be plenty of men in the State Department who don't like what you're doing in Vietnam. Your setup is called the Establishment, ours the Party."

As I listened to this man of unmistakable integrity wrestling with his problem and his conscience, I was touched. It occurred to me that in the West any number of young idealists have moved from rebellion to a comfortable place in the establishment, and I wondered how many young Soviet men and women who were remaining aloof from their establishment would eventually accept rewarding roles in it.

17

In the City

ALTHOUGH MGU was largely self-contained, its denizens went into the city on a variety of missions—to attend classes at downtown faculties, to seek entertainment, to get a change of pace in dining, to shop in big department stores like GUM (the Macy's of Moscow) to visit nonuniversity acquaintances, and occasionally to obtain certain services that were, at least in theory, more expeditious downtown.

Consider dry cleaning. The university had its own facilities in the basement, but service was slow and bewildering. The time had come, after a long Moscow winter in which I had lived in three suits, to seek help from the dry cleaner. But at MGU the process took more than a week and what was utterly disheartening was that the customer was instructed to remove all buttons before submitting his clothes to the machines. Button, button, where's the button? All over an American's suits. I would not have believed it, but when I made a careful count, I found seven buttons on each jacket—two per cuff and three down the Ivy League front—and eight on each pair of pants. That made a total of fifteen on each suit, not counting the vest, which I quickly decided didn't need cleaning. With three suits—still leaving the vests to fend for themselves—I was confronted by the staggering chore of removing forty-five buttons and then having to sew them on again. Even if I were adept at sewing, which I am not, I would have turned heaven and earth for a simpler way out.

Eureka! So I thought. I heard that there were three stores in Moscow that use American-made machines to clean clothes in one day and, miracle of miracles, with the buttons on. At the first scent of spring, which in Moscow's austere climate came late in April, I set off for one of these stores.

It was quite early in the morning when I arrived at the door—that is to say, I judged there must be a door at the end of the long line of customers that snaked across the sidewalk and into the street. Through the glass store front I could see the bulky American dry cleaning machines and a batch of American self-service washers and dryers as well. I could also make out four different lines of customers which were, as I later found out, Number 1 to leave dirty clothes, Number 2 to pick up clean ones, Number 3 to leave shirts, and Number 4 to the self-service machines.

The longest line, naturally, was mine. Chatting with my Russian companions on line I learned that the store had been accepting soiled garments for some time and was approaching the limit of its morning Plan. The norm was two hundred fifty *shtook*—items—since the machines could handle no more than that and still clean everything in twenty-four hours. Pardoning my way through the lines, I reached the counter and was informed by a harried clerk that the store would accept one hundred fifty more *shtook* that morning. After that, no more *shtook* until 5:00 P.M., when the store would begin on its afternoon quota of two hundred fifty items.

I reported what I had learned to my line, which was made up mainly of *starushkas* with a sprinkling of younger people. Everyone agreed it would be fruitless to wait, that one might spend two hours, reach the counter, and turn out to be the owner of *shtooka* number 251. But nobody left the line. A young man who needed a shave and kept consulting his watch said this was his third attempt in three days to reach the counter and this time, "*Chiort voz'mi* (Devil take it)," he would stay. A young woman with long hair piled prettily on her head looked progressively more worried. A little old lady smiled benevolently as two other *starushkas* quarreled over their position in line.

"Let them fight," she said philosophically. "It gives them something to do while they wait."

And so we stood for an hour. Then, as we approached the crowded, stuffy vestibule, the girl accepting garments behind the counter called out portentously, "*Prinimaiutsia eshcho sto shtook* (one hundred *shtook* to go)." I decided to take action. I began to canvass the customers.

"How many *shtook* do you have?" I asked each person in line. Some laughed, and some were momentarily taken aback, but everyone obediently made a count of his burden of *shtook*. Soon my comrades-in-waiting were smiling and calling out encouragement. "Isn't he scientific?" murmured a *starushka* admiringly.

I counted thirty people ahead of me carrying ninety *shtook*. In other words, I would just make it. But I had forgotten two pivotal facts. One was that Russian lines widen faster than they lengthen. The second was even more deadly. What exactly was a *shtooka?* Was a suit considered one or two? When I fought my way to the counter again, I learned to my dismay that it was two.

It was now nearly 1:00 P.M., and I admitted defeat. Half the *starushkas* of Russia, it seemed, had joined their friends ahead of me. I took my three suits with their forty-five buttons and retreated to the dorm.

At 5:00 P.M. I was back. Again the line was the first thing I saw as I approached the store. It was just as long as it had been at 1:00 P.M. I was about to depart, meditating the prospect of three more months in clothes that would soon walk away by themselves, or the more odious prospect of removing the forty-five buttons, when I spied familiar faces inside. My morning companions were now at the head of the line. They had been rejected at 2:00 P.M., but one enterprising man had made a list of the two o'clock losers so they could lead the line at five. Though I had fled too soon to make the list, my scientific survey, even more than my face, was remembered, and I was invited to take the eleventh position from the counter.

By now the customers in line behind me were mainly men and women on their way home from work. But even my morning friends looked different. The young man mounting his third assault on the cleaners had shaved. The young woman had let down her hair, curled it, covered it with a kerchief, and picked up a daughter at nursery school. And the *starushka* who had chuckled indulgently at the morning's quarrel was now battling over a place in line herself.

This time I waited thirty minutes before giving up my suits, paying eight rubles in advance and taking a place in another line waiting to use the self-service machines. Next I did my laundry—a thirty-minute job after another thirty-minute wait—and I was ready to go home. Only one problem remained. Chatting with a neighbor, I learned the clerk had overcharged me for the suits. At the risk of being lynched, I pushed my way to the head of line Number 1 and asked for a recount. Since the clerk was clearly wrong, the people in line were patient and sympathetic. At 7:00 P.M. I lurched through the crowd still on the sidewalk and headed home. The last thing I heard was someone shouting "Seventy *shtook* to go!"

Picking up my suits the next day was an anticlimax. There was no one on line Number 2. It was a breeze—my suits were handsomely cleaned and all forty-five buttons in place, not one to be sewed on.

My day at the dry cleaners had a certain charm for me. It even touched my dissertation topic, since the municipal government runs dry cleaning establishments. But for the Russians on line the long wait was no joke; it clearly took a heavy toll in time and energy.

"Somebody ought to complain about the service," one of my companions on line had grumbled toward the evening the first day. But the young man who finally made it on his third try was more cynical. "After wasting this much time," he muttered, "who's got the time to complain?"

Throughout my stay in Moscow I seized every opportunity to talk with Russians everywhere, with those I met on lines, with salesgirls, cleaning ladies, waiters, taxi drivers, clerks, teachers, and laborers of all sorts. At MGU itself there were hundreds of men and women who were in the university but not of it—sales personnel and petty functionaries in stores and *stolovaias*. They worked long hours at low pay and knew that students looked down on them and their jobs. Little wonder then that salesgirls doled out goods so dourly, that waitresses served so slowly, that cashiers made change so grudgingly, or that a woman called "The Screamer" administered the trunk room as though her life depended on keeping students' trunks out of it. Of course there were pleasant souls, like the woman at the grocery store who gave me a bottle of cream when I asked for a bottle of milk, saying that I needed to put on weight. But when the subject was service, my Russian friends groused about the grumpy servants of the state who, they said, mellowed only after you asked for the complaint book, which was checked periodically by supervisors.

I would have given a great deal to attend a meeting once advertised in the MGU grocery store. The broad-beamed *prodavshchitsy*—salesladies—and the red-faced young men who dragged crates of milk bottles in and out were to be briefed on the Twenty-third Party Congress. I tried to imagine them, the glum givers of fish, the sullen slicers of sausage, the amiable arbiters of eggs, all wrapped in their dirty white aprons questioning a Party lecturer on subjects of moment like the tasks of literature and the Chinese situation. I never found out what happened at that meeting. Once I had tried to get into a meeting of student agitators not open to the public, only to be stopped at the door by an official who was agitated that I was a foreign student. This time I didn't even try. *Nichevo!* If I couldn't pass as an agitator, I sure as hell couldn't make it as a *prodavshchitsa.*

My friends spoke of people doing humble chores as *Prostye liudi*—simple people—or peasants at heart, and assured me that I would learn nothing from them. I suspect my friends would not have admired the near-sighted *babushka* who worked in the laundry room and washed my shirts for me. Accustomed to students with one or two shirts, she marveled that I always had several dirty ones to leave when I picked up clean ones. The wonder of it was so great that it never ceased to amaze her. Nor would my friends have appreciated the begrimed female street cleaner who wandered up with her short black broom when I was displaying a Kennedy half dollar to a pleasant elderly lady in a Moscow park. The lady had begun the park bench conversation by warning me I would catch my death of cold if I didn't wear a hat. Hearing I was an American—I had said Americans aren't used to wearing heavy fur hats—she told me the Soviet people had greatly admired President Kennedy. She shuddered therefore when the simple street cleaner stared at the likeness of Kennedy and allowed with a grunt of recognition that it was a portrait of Stalin.

"Oh, no," cried the lady. "That's not Stalin. That's the late American President Kennedy, whom we admired so much."

The sweeper extracted some ancient eyeglasses from a pocket of her sooty smock and squinted at the coin.

"Are you sure it's not Stalin?" she asked.

"No, it is not Stalin!" snapped the good woman, embarrassed and angry.

"Well," the street cleaner shook her head slowly, "it certainly looks like Stalin."

That was too much. Trembling with anger, the lady shooed away the sweeper, then apologized to me.

"You must not judge the Soviet people by her. She is a very simple woman."

"Mir i druzhba (Peace and friendship)," muttered the retreating sweeper.

"You see," said the lady, softening, "even our *prostye liudi* are for peace."

As I bade her good-bye, she reminded me to wear a hat. The next day I followed her advice, only to be reproached on the street by another unfamiliar old woman who said, "If you wear such a heavy hat now, young man, what will you wear when it is really cold?" Both bits of unsolicited advice were typical. As far as I could see, *babushkas* specialized in (1) reprimanding other people's grandchildren who carve their initials on frosted bus windows, "Study a lot—learn a little," (2) lecturing army officers who kiss their wives in full view of other passengers in the metro, "Have you no respect for your uniform, *tovarishch?*" (3) condemning a man who permits his dog to sit on the front seat of his car, "That *molodoi chelovek* (young man), is a disgraceful display of affluence," (4) advising perfect strangers to put on, but never to take off, weight, and (5) detecting and berating students who, for a short bus ride, travel *zaichikom*—like a little rabbit—that is, without paying the fare.

One evening I found myself in a group of *starushkas* on a downtown sidewalk staring through a café's picture window at young people twisting and frugging.

"Nenormal'no!" muttered an old lady.

"Prosto nekul'turno!" complained another.

"Nazyvaetsia swist (It's called the 'swist')," grumbled a third. *"Bezobrazie* (What an outrage)!"

A hip young Russian emerged from the café.

"It's called the 'twist,' not the 'swist,' *babusi* (grannies)," he twitted them. "And you're just jealous because you don't know how to do it."

Although my Russian friends were sometimes irritated by nosy *babushkas,* I found them endlessly amusing.

Taxi drivers in Moscow as everywhere else in the world were unreconstructed characters, informative, amusing, and maddening. Some students regarded cabbies—and waiters, too—as lumpen proletariat bent on shirking productive work. I found them alert and, as soon as they learned I was an American, curious about life in America. Like the students, they made their points tactfully, asking if the unflattering things they read in their newspapers were really true. Many had harsh words for their own press ("You can't believe much you read in this country. How about the U.S.A.?"); for the Plan ("The damn Plan makes us return to the garage just when people are coming out of theaters"); and for political education ("In the army all we had to do to get top grades in political instruction was to say 'America Stinks.'").

One chap was implacably pessimistic. "Life is terrible here," he said. "I live in one room with my wife and son. How can my boy do his homework at night? It's a disgrace."

"Perhaps things will be getting better," I said to comfort a fellow creature.

"No. It won't get any better."

"Well, I guess life is rough," I said.

"You call this living?"

But others, staunch champions of the Soviet way of life, assured me that all was well and getting better, that education was free and so was medical care and how could you ask people to pay for either? Did I realize that the miles of new apartment houses we were passing had all been built since the end of World War II? And how could I explain America's losing that hydrogen bomb in Spain, or how could anyone justify killing women and children in Vietnam?

"Who needs war?" asked a broad-shouldered driver wearing an old army jacket. "We know what war is like. I lost my father and brother. My family went hungry. We ate garbage and grass. Just look how far our country has come since then."

Again and again I was beseeched by humble people to transmit a message: "Tell the American people we don't ever want to fight them." Sometimes the comment was shorter: *"Mir i druzhba."* My MGU friends shunned the phrase as cliché; *prostye liudi* repeated it with such sincerity that it didn't sound hackneyed. "War brings only sorrow and pain," said a weary, sad-faced woman who drove a taxi twelve hours every other day to support a husband made an invalid by the war. "Nobody knows the grief of a mother with no food for a child who is hungry."

Knowing how Russians felt about war, I studied the faces of those who gathered on May Day to watch the parade of awesome weapons of war. It was a brisk, sunny morning, the kind you'd meet in New York in November, and I couldn't help thinking of Macy's Thanksgiving Day parade as I watched Russian families, the parents leading children holding flowers and balloons. There were few policemen to be seen on the avenue, which was some distance from Red Square, and when the parade came into view the crowd pressed forward, leaving only a narrow lane in the middle of the street. The lethal behemoths that rumbled through the narrow lane were terrifying to behold: block-long intercontinental ballistic missiles, heavy tanks, rocket launchers, and huge armored troop carriers filled with helmeted troops. Yet no one in the crowd retreated before the thunderous din and the pall of exhaust, and a few dashed between the ICBM's like kids daring to approach an enormous Mickey Mouse float. I saw no fear in Russian faces but sensed no exultation.

I had the same sensation on November 7 as I watched the military parade in honor of the Revolution's anniversary in a group of foreigners standing just outside Red Square. When the massed populace marched by after the tanks and rockets had gone, we climbed over the barriers and, just for kicks, joined the demonstration. Our "detachment" consisted of workers from a local factory, and once among them we found that they were not marching, but dancing, prancing, singing, and staggering their way through Red Square. It was New Year's Eve all over again. By the time we passed under the benevolent gaze of the Party leaders atop Lenin's mausoleum, a foreigner was carrying a huge Soviet flag that the Soviet bearer was too tipsy to handle. The blown-up portraits of Soviet leaders so familiar from news pictures turned out to be mounted on two-wheeled frames, which teen-age boys propelled like soapbox chariots. I felt as if I were in the middle of a weird Surrealist happening. There were the omnipotent Brezhnev and Kosygin in the flesh, smiling down on us, while two lads, like Roman charioteers, raced enormous likenesses of the great men.

As an American I had unexpected and illuminating encounters with strangers. One day in the Restaurant Moskva I met a young plumber from Sverdlovsk who had come into town that day on his first visit. Because the restaurant was crowded, I took an empty seat at his table—an accepted custom in the Soviet Union. When he asked me about life in Moscow, I broke it to him that I was not from Moscow either.

"From America!" he exclaimed and quickly poured me a glass of wine. "I've always had two dreams—to study law at night school and to visit America."

I was the first American he had ever met. When I told him, in response to his barrage of questions, that American plumbers made as much as six dollars an hour, and that the average American worker makes about $5,000 a year, he was downright angry. "Why don't they tell us those things about America?" he said. "We can take it. We'll still be proud of our country." He asked me to write my New York address in his book. "Not because I'll ever get there," he said. "But it'll be fun to have an American's address."

He was clearly sincere. But Moscow has a small army of flatterers. It is made up of *stiliagi*—sharpies—who hang around the tourist hotels, approach Americans, and profess embarrassingly profuse admiration for America and bitter disillusionment with their own country. Some seek only sympathy; others ask to buy your shirt at black market prices. My madras jacket was a real prize, as I discovered one day when a zoot-suited young Russian stopped me on the street and handed me the following note: "I am deaf and dumb. I will buy your jacket for forty rubles."

Occasionally Russian friends invited me to their homes in Moscow. Not many, because some Russians are fearful and others are reluctant to entertain in a small crowded flat shared by parents and perhaps even grandparents. Naturally one would not expect a dinner invitation from a casual acquaintance in the United States and one is even less likely to get it in Moscow. Thanks to these visits, I discovered some interesting facts. Cooperative apartments are better built than state-owned buildings. A resourceful housewife can order groceries on the phone and have them delivered to her door without ever standing in the lines I knew so well. It is rare to see new apartments with more than three or four rooms. But when I visited a highly-placed Party personage, I found he had six rooms and in them were such amenities as a Western tape recorder, Western phonograph, Western records, and a Soviet washing machine. As hosts in their homes, Russians were warm and outgoing. One evening after a housewarming party in a mathematician's new apartment, a group of us—I was the only American—marched down Leninskii Prospekt singing in English "The Battle Hymn of the Republic."

I had a chance to spend an evening at one of Moscow's special middle schools where classes are conducted in English.

I had been invited to sing American folk songs, but I was more entertained than entertaining. The evening had been arranged by the *Klub interesnykh vstrech*—Club of Interesting Meetings—which meets periodically with "interesting guests." As an officially designated "interesting guest" I was met on the front steps by the welcoming committee and ushered into an auditorium arranged like Symphony Hall for a Boston Pops concert: a stage at one end and tables set with food and drink. The first performers were *ucheniki*—pupils. Three girls sang the club song, a catchy number entitled appropriately *"Klub interesnykh vstrech,"* which had been composed by a ten-year-old who found time between opening and closing the curtain to tell me that he had also composed fifteen other pieces. Next was a skit lampooning the school uniform; a boy played a movement from a Mozart piano sonata; and then it was time for the "interesting guests." Four young men and four young women from a Sports Institute demonstrated the latest social dances which featured not the twist but "The Hill of Coal," a creation of their own, which looked suspiciously like the Lindy to me. Next we heard from a formidable female, a tough, gravel-voiced geographer who had lived in Siberia and Africa and who recalled the ferocious beasts she had met and no doubt intimidated. *"Dorogie deti* (Dear children). When I reached this great, green continent of Africa, I realized that I am not only a citizen of our great country, but also a citizen of the world. Now, thanks to the triumphs of Soviet cosmonauts, I am a citizen of the cosmos as well."

I was next. *"Dorogie deti,"* I began. The *ucheniki* laughed, and after that it was easy. I sang "This Land Is Your Land" and "Clementine," but the students cried out that those songs were too old, and could I sing "Blowing in the Wind" and "We Shall Overcome." Happily I could, and when I did, some *ucheniki* produced guitars and sang along.

On occasion I visited museums with MGU friends, and we

overheard comments which obviously embarrassed them. While following a party of workers around the big exhibition of the Art of the Baltic Republics, we heard them scoff at "Spring in the World," a mildly stylized painting of a youthful soldier in a lush green forest. "It should be called," muttered one onlooker, " 'Where the Hell Am I?' " A painting of a nude, extravagantly rounded milkmaid in a meadow produced snickers and the comment, "I never saw a collective farm like that." But in the presence of a large canvas of Lenin and his masses, the group stood admiringly, and we heard a worker exclaim, "Now that's what I call real art!"

Once I wandered into a lecture in a downtown library. The topic was alienation. At MGU such a provocative subject would have sparked fireworks. I wondered what would happen in this gathering of middle-aged citizens, mostly women.

"Alienation," said the speaker, a lady professor of philosophy, "is a phenomenon of capitalist society. There can be no alienation in a socialist society where men are united by patriotism, internationalism, and the struggle to build Communism."

She spoke so earnestly that I was sure she believed every word she uttered.

At question time a young man, one of the few young people in the audience, spoke up. "Are you quite sure," he asked thoughtfully, "that there is no alienation in our society?"

That was the kind of question I could count on at MGU, but I did not expect it here.

"There can be no alienation in a socialist society."

And that was that. There were no more questions.

"Let's see the film," came the cry from all sides, and in a moment they were happily watching "Soviet Singers at La Scala."

In the corridor, the lecturer stood in a small circle.

"We have it here, too." said a gaunt, hollow-eyed young man. "You can see it in the eyes of drunks. You can sense it in the silent struggle for success. You can hear it in the complaints of those who failed. You can find it in giant, impersonal factories and universities."

The lecturer, a severe but comely woman of about fifty, suddenly seemed sad and very tired. "Perhaps you're right," she sighed. "But it's not really alienation. It can't be the same thing that exists under capitalism. We have no system of private property forcing men to act like cannibals. Don't forget the way we struggled together to build up this country in the thirties and again after the war. Don't forget the beautiful moments of life and nature and art, the simple human commitment that can inspire us."

"What about Sinyavsky and Daniel?" continued the young man. "Aren't they alienated? Instead of attacking them, we should ask ourselves what in our society alienated such good, intelligent men."

"I see no justification for what they did," the professor snapped. "They got what they deserved."

"But Voznesensky, too, published work abroad and received payment," put in a young woman.

The gaunt young man nodded.

"All I can say is that if we don't give our writers more freedom, we'll have more like Sinyavsky and Daniel."

Standing on the edge of the circle, I said nothing, and they paid no attention to me. As I turned to go, the sound track of "Soviet Singers at La Scala" could be heard through the door. At the end of the corridor, I looked back. The discussion was still animated. Off the campus, too, Russians were troubled and asking questions.

18

In the Provinces

AT THE HEIGHT of one of MGU's most tumultuous Party lectures, a Party speaker lashed out irritably at his hostile audience: "You know, we don't get this kind of reception outside of Moscow. People are more polite there."

Soviet friends from the provinces agreed. "Moscow is a special case," one said. "People ask more questions here because they see more contrasts. Moscow has more Western culture, more Western cars, and more Western tourists than any other city. These give Muscovites an exaggerated notion of the West's wealth that doesn't jibe with what they read in the press. And there are a lot of well-to-do Russians in Moscow. There are fewer contrasts in the hinterlands and hence fewer questions."

Is this true? At various times and for various periods I have visited Erevan, Tbilisi, Yalta, Vladimir, Yaroslavl, Piatigorsk, Donetsk, Zaporozh'e, Kharkov, Kiev, Riga, Leningrad, and Novgorod. Anyone who tries to make cosmic generalizations after visits of any duration anywhere is presumptuous, but some impressions may be pertinent and valid. Whether I traveled with or without official guides, I had opportunities for moments of illumination.

I found that interest in America and in all things American was higher than in Moscow. In 1964 it was difficult for thirty Russian-speaking Americans touring together not to draw attention to themselves like so many magnets. We were stared at, followed, and besieged with questions. On my own I attracted much less notice. There was little obviously American about me, or so I thought. My clothes were Muscovite—fur-collared overcoat and fur hat—and my Russian was secure. Only a few natives doubted that I was a Soviet citizen; the only question was which part of the country I came from. More often than not I was pegged as a resident of a Baltic Republic. But when people realized that I was an American—and I made a point of telling them so—the conversation turned to the U.S.A. and stayed there, if I let it.

The conversation stayed there for more hours than I care to recall in the Ukrainian mining center of Donetsk. At a Komsomol youth club, young doctors, engineers, and workers peppered me with questions about American prices, mores, and politics until I ran out of energy. I thought of excusing myself at midnight, but they insisted on walking me back to my hotel and even took the long way to prolong the discussion. At 1:00 A.M. a *druzhinnik*—auxiliary policeman—approached our strolling talkative company, which had swelled to about thirty as it ambled through the darkened streets toward the hotel. It was un-Soviet activity, he said, to stand around chattering at an hour when citizens should be asleep, preparing for the next day's work. My new friends ignored him. At 2:00 A.M. I found myself standing on the front steps of the hotel explaining one last time, like a hoarse-voiced tribune, that it was not inconceivable that one man acting alone might have assassinated the President of the United States.

Compared with my MGU friends, young people I met on the road seemed modest, even humble. They apologized in advance for not knowing more about the United States. Although MGU students admitted that they knew too little about America, they blamed the Soviet press. In the provinces people blamed the provinces. "We don't really keep up with things out here," apologized a *studentka* at the Yaroslavl Pedagogical Institute. "This isn't Moscow, you know."

Many had never encountered an American before. Their demeanor was scrupulously polite. They took pains to be flattering about the U.S.A. and I, in turn, was equally gallant. When asked, as I invariably was, how I liked the Soviet Union, I replied, *"Sovsem ne plokho* (very not bad)." Some were pleased; they seemed to accept my response at face value. Others, more sophisticated, assured me that they would not be offended if I criticized. One chap, a mud-spattered workman on a road gang in the small Caucasian spa of Kislovodsk, dropped his shovel and exclaimed, *"Sovsem ne plokho?* You're joking. You mean things aren't better in America?"

In the provinces, as in Moscow, people went out of their way, even in the briefest encounters, to tell me that they knew all too well what war was like and never wanted it again. Many asked me to convey that message to the American people, and what was most touching was that simple Russians singled out Americans in their own calling, as if they would understand the message. Taxi drivers sent greetings to American taxi drivers. Peasants I met on a collective farm near Zaporozh'e wanted their words carried to American farmers. Once as I was crawling along the bottom of a Donetsk coal mine 1,200 feet below the surface—we had been invited to tour the tunnels in miners' outfits supplied by the management—I met some soot-blackened men groping through the gloom.

"Americans?" A miner echoed our guide incredulously. "Tell the American miners that we want to live at peace with them."

Western jazz and the twist, uncrowned kings of MGU parties, were only upstarts in the provinces. At Kharkov University, students wanted to hear American folk songs but declined, in some embarrassment, to twist. So did young people in Piatigorsk, Vladimir, Zaporozh'e, and Novgorod. But in Yalta, the Black Sea watering spot where Soviet vacationers let down their hair, jazz filled the sea front. From the outdoor dance halls in Yuri Gagarin Park of Culture and Rest it drifted, familiar Western sounds alternating with a softer Soviet kind of music. In an outdoor movie theater just off the boardwalk, a musical comedy made in Azerbaijan reached a twice-nightly crescendo with Chubby Checker screaming "Let's Twist Again Like We Did Last Summer." And several strollers on the crowded promenade had shortwave transistors tuned in on the Voice of America. I had thought that MGU students were taking chances in listening so openly to the V.O.A.; but in Yalta, on the boardwalk, three teen-agers turned up their set so high that they immediately drew a crowd. Boys on the beach stopped skipping flat stones across the water and came over to listen. So did vacationers who had been watching an artist do "cut out silhouetted profiles while you wait," and so did five girls who had been morosely contemplating a bulletin predicting rain the next day. When a policeman approached, I feared the worst; but he leaned against the lamppost and listened with the rest of them to V.O.A.'s report of news of the day.

Not everyone in the provinces displayed friendly interest in America. Komsomol activists were more dogmatic and combative than those I knew at MGU. If they were eager to meet Americans, it was because they wanted to take them on in aggressive debate. They did not ask if the disparaging picture of America in the Soviet press "was really true"; they assumed it was, and they actually tried to convince an American of the reliability of their facts. Indignantly they recited the litany: racial oppression, rampant unemployment, atrocities in Vietnam. With an air of lofty self-righteousness they asked a visitor to compare the gloomy prospects of capitalism with the brilliant future of Communism. Yet they were sensitive to the smallest slight. How did they explain Stalinism? Stalin, they explained parrot-like, was responsible for grave blunders; but it was necessary to remember his important contributions. Poor harvests in agriculture? Basically due to unpropitious climatic conditions. Unopposed candidates in Soviet elections? The Soviet people, they insisted, were united. Hungary? The Soviet Union had put down a fascist counterrevolution. This kind of sparring was a bore, but once it paid unexpected dividends. I met a strikingly beautiful girl in Zaporozh'e who turned out to be a devout *komsomolka.* I wanted to ask her for a date. I thought of suggesting a stroll in the park or a movie, but I feared that she would say no. At least I could hope for a long causerie—and got it. So long as I plied her with challenging questions about Soviet life she felt she had no alternative but to stand her ground and respond.

In the provinces, as in Moscow, rigidly didactic activists were a minority. Most young people did not preach the virtues of their system or criticize it. If pressed, they would defend, though not vehemently; but their first instinct was to avoid controversy. They were not likely to speak up for the quality of Soviet housing, but they would defend the uses of socialist realism in art and literature. When we sang Russian songs, they did not attempt underground numbers, and I wondered whether they were familiar with them. Several times I suggested Okudzhava songs only to have them propose "Moscow Nights," the venerable favorite that my MGU friends considered passé.

People this cautious were not likely to invite a touring American to their homes, nor would they meet him in his hotel. They did not volunteer their last names or telephone numbers, and they even looked over their shoulders in public places. One could almost sense the painful ambivalence. Eager to meet an American, but at the same time afraid, they were nervous. When I later recounted these conversations to MGU friends, they told me not to take the cool reception personally, or even entirely as a reaction to an American, though, of course, hobnobbing with foreigners and especially with Americans was not the most acceptable Soviet pastime. People in the provinces, they said, could be almost as wary and in awe of Russians from Moscow. A student recalled the Komsomol junket he made through the hinterlands—how local people had kept their distance from what they thought was a high-powered *delegatsia* carrying an identifying letter from the Central Committee of the Komsomol. They did not realize that the *delegatsia* was not taking itself seriously and that it was displaying its imposing letter partly in fun and partly to cut through red tape. Another MGU friend recounted the story, perhaps apocryphal, of the *starik* in a small Siberian town who was awakened in the dead of night by a call from the Moscow authorities, who wanted to know if he had relatives in France.

"Oh, no," said the old man, remembering the time when having relatives abroad was a sign of sedition. "Not I. None at all. Never."

Only when Moscow explained that rich relatives reported to be his had died and left him a large sum of freely exchangeable French francs did he confess his kinship.

The exceptions to the general mood of caution were university students who, as in Moscow, seemed more informal, freer, and more questioning. In Kharkov I was asked what I was studying in the United States, and when I told them that Communist ideology was one of my subjects, they were aghast.

"Why do you bother? We spend our time trying to avoid it."

During a boat ride along the Black Sea coast, two Soviet

students provided me with an impudent counterpoint to the running commentary of a grandfather to a tow-headed grandson.

"See that, Aliosha," said the old man, pointing to a radar installation on a cliff. "That's to keep out smugglers and enemy saboteurs."

"And to keep Russians from swimming to Turkey," whispered my friend.

"And that, Aliosha," said *dedushka*—grandfather—turning to a glass building on the edge of the water, "is the house Khrushchev built for his vacations. Inside is a swimming pool."

"Poor Nikita Sergeevich," murmured my friend. "He never had time to learn to swim before they ousted him."

Finally, high on a green bluff, the old man spied the Tsar's palace where Roosevelt, Churchill, and Stalin had deliberated early in 1945.

"Now it's a sanatorium for the workers." The old man beamed.

"Not in the summer," growled my friend. "That's when *nachal'stvo* (management) takes it over."

At Armenia's Erevan State University, the dormitory was old, peeling, and crowded—a far cry from luxurious MGU. But the students had much the same concerns on their minds as those in Moscow.

"The older generation cannot understand us," said one chap bitterly.

"Every country has a problem of generations," replied a girl. "Misunderstandings are natural. The people on top ought to recognize that instead of denying there is a problem."

Did I think that Soviet students were more idealistic than Americans? Before I could answer there was an interruption:

"What do you mean by Soviet ideals? How many can you name?"

Like their colleagues at MGU, Erevan students prided themselves on being realistic.

"I guess you'll have to compromise," a student told me. "Even if you happen to admire anything in our system, you'll have to attack us when you get home."

I objected that this was not so, but although he didn't believe me, he tried to be comforting. "We understand. It happens here, too. You've got to compromise to live."

The farther one gets from Moscow the more freely people speak. I found that they spoke most freely of all in non-Russian areas, Latvia on the Baltic and in Georgia and Armenia near the Black Sea.

On a flight from Kiev to Riga I sat next to a Latvian woman who complained from takeoff to touch-down. Although Khrushchev was still in power in 1964, she ridiculed "that boor" more cuttingly than MGU students did after his fall. A friend of hers—a Russian woman—looked grim, especially when the Latvian woman agreed to meet me the next day to show me around Riga. The next morning the complainer did not show.

In Tbilisi, which is a thousand miles from Moscow, compared to Riga's five hundred, Georgians did not hesitate to meet alone with an American. And when they did, they spoke rapturously of their native green, rich Georgia, comparing it patronizingly to other places in the Soviet Union. Tbilisi struck me as a little bit of Paris in the Soviet south. Residents dressed more stylishly than Muscovites—women looked smart in print dresses, sometimes worn teasingly off the shoulder; and men, with dark hair and inevitable mustaches, cut dashing figures. Store windows were arranged with a special flair, and inside there were fewer lines than in Moscow. Even the cops were sharper as they directed traffic from streamlined glass booths high above the street. I recalled Lenin's formula that "Communism equals Soviet power plus electrification," and thought to myself that a little Georgification wouldn't hurt either.

Typical of Tbilisi hospitality was the reception I received at the Institute of Marxism-Leninism of the Academy of Sciences. In Moscow I had been denied entrance to much less august establishments, but here a deputy director and several scholars dropped everything to welcome me.

I asked one for an explanation of Georgia's abundance.

"The climate and the good rich earth," he said, "but socialism is part of it, too. Without Soviet power I would still be a peasant." A pause, and he continued. "Still, I'm glad I was once a peasant and not a city boy. I don't believe in God now, but I once did. And I still wonder when I walk alone in a meadow on a starlit night."

Once I strolled along a river that meanders through the suburbs of Erevan and paused to ask directions of steel-workers picnicking on the grass. When I identified myself as American, they instantly cleared a place and insisted that I partake of the shaslik cooking on an open fire. "You're in Erevan now, not Moscow," said one black-browed Armenian. I found myself staring at a tattoo of Stalin on a worker's arm, and he felt compelled to explain, "We took down the statue of Stalin in the city." He spit in the general direction of the departed statue's massive stone base, which can be seen for miles around, then pointed to the tattoo again. "But this won't come off."

If the people I met in Erevan were informal, so were the four men who followed me night and day everywhere I went. When I left the picnickers and continued my hike, they rose from a shady spot under a tree on the other side of the river and continued theirs. When I reached a main highway and hopped aboard a bus, they jumped into a waiting car. And for the rest of my stay they didn't even bother to change the car. At 6:00 A.M. on the morning I was to leave Erevan I sat in the airport, casually glanced out the window into the murky parking lot, and saw them sitting there—in the only car in the lot.

I had been warned by Westerners in Moscow that an American traveling alone might expect interesting propositions, but it wasn't until Erevan that I got the call—from a husky female voice on the telephone.

"Is this that nice American?" she asked sweetly in English.

In the best Russian I could muster I replied, "I don't understand the language you're speaking."

"This is a nice girl you would like to meet," she said in English.

"Nu, eto neponiatno (Well, I don't understand)," I said, and hung up.

Had she been working for the same people who hired the men in the car? Later a friend at Intourist told me she might have been "an independent."

My experiences in Moscow with the little men in brown suits had prepared me for obvious tailing. But what happened in Yaroslavl was absurdly clumsy. I was getting into a taxi to head for the railroad station when a breathless Russian in a trench coat came running up and grabbed me by the arm.

"Where are you going?" he pleaded.

I had never seen him before and I asked politely why he wanted to know.

"Nado znat! (I have to know!)"

He was so forlorn that I told him.

If there were any secret policemen on the train from Yaroslavl to Moscow, they were cleverly disguised as soldiers in long underwear with feet wrapped in rags, or as peasants and workers in pajamas. The train had set out from the Siberian end of the Trans-Siberian Railroad eight days earlier, and the passengers sitting or sleeping on triple-decker bunks looked as if they had been aboard since Gogol had created them. The windows were closed to keep out soot from the engine, the air was foul, and the rest rooms were unspeakable. (If nations are judged by the state of their public toilets, as an MGU law professor suggested they might be, then the U.S.S.R. is in troubled waters, so to speak.) In private compartments at the far end of the train were well-to-do Russians and foreign tourists and, at first, I wished I were with them. But my weary companions, despite their week in transit, or perhaps because of it, were so relaxed that they welcomed Americans with more warmth and informality than anyone else I met in the provinces.

"What will it be like to live under full Communism?" a jovial Armenian asked aloud, and then answered himself. "I'll tell you. Everyone's wife will be mine. From each according to ability, to me according to my need."

His neighbors, a grizzled old man and a sloppy young one, said they would drink to that, and they did.

"I'll tell you Americans how to drink," said the old man. "Slowly, that's how."

"Absoliutno verno (Absolutely true)," the young man responded.

"You've got to eat when you drink or you won't see straight," the old man elaborated for everyone's edification.

"Absoliutno verno," echoed his younger colleague.

"Little Pioneers drink like this," the old man continued relentlessly, holding two fingers a jigger's length apart. "For *komsomoltsy,"* he spread his fingers a little more. "And for the Party member," it was *do dna.* He gave the international gesture for bottoms up.

As the train neared Moscow, passengers trooped to the bathroom to get dressed or pulled on clothes over their pajamas, then busied themselves with stowing their belongings into suitcases and duffel bags. The music that had been coming over the loudspeaker gave way to a sugary female voice wishing us "Welcome to Moscow, Capital of the Union of Soviet Socialist Republics." Just before the train stopped, two peasant women asked me how to get from the station to Red Square, and I gave them directions. In the depot, the Soviet provincials picked up their children and gear and, looking apprehensive, headed into the big city.

19

In East Europe

I WANTED to visit some other Communist countries on my way home from Moscow. The logical route was through Eastern Europe, but why not China? The idea popped into my head in the fall of 1965 as I looked out my MGU window and gazed at the Chinese Embassy. Probably there wasn't a chance, but you couldn't lose by trying. After all, I was part of the way to Peking. Just to see what would happen, I decided to pursue it as if I did have a chance.

I began by applying to the American Embassy for permission. It was an unusual request, because the State Department had not yet liberalized its rule to permit scholars and others with a legitimate interest to travel to China. The Embassy promised nothing, but it didn't say no.

The next step was to the Chinese Embassy to ask for a visa. But what kind of reception would an American get from the Chinese? What indeed would Soviet authorities think of an American who went knocking at their unfriendly ally's door? Would the MGU squad of brown-suited men tail me? What would be the reaction from Soviet policemen standing guard at the Embassy gate?

The Chinese Embassy stands, ironically, on Friendship Among Peoples Street. Although I could see it from my room, it was five minutes away by taxi. The morning I arrived, the street, which boiled with Soviet demonstrations against the Chinese in 1967, was deserted except for three Soviet police sentries wearing greatcoats, fur hats and holstered pistols. I asked one where to enter the building, half-expecting him to stop me, but he merely saluted, just as policemen in front of the American Embassy invariably did, and pointed to the side door. Walking across the broad circle drive, which had been cleared of snow, I looked back for my old security friends. None was visible.

The man who came to the door of the consular section was young and slender, wearing a high-buttoned blue tunic. There was no one else in sight.

"May I help you?" he asked in Russian.

"I would like to obtain a visa to visit China as a tourist," I replied in Russian.

He looked me up and down, at my fur hat and fur-collared overcoat wondering, no doubt, why a Russian wanted to visit China in this period of Sino-Soviet tension.

I decided to level with him immediately. "I am an American student, studying at MGU."

"I see," he said mildly. He invited me inside and showed me into a large waiting room just past the vestibule. "Wait here, please," he said, then closed the door and left.

The room, flooded with sunlight which poured in through a picture window, contained a luxurious leather sofa, three deep leather chairs, a large oval mahogany coffee table, and, along the wall, some exquisitely filigreed wooden chairs and a cabinet with several lovely Chinese vases. Did the room also boast hidden microphones? If so, who was bugging whom? Russians the Chinese? Chinese the Russians? Or each the other?

I waited nearly thirty minutes before the door opened again and an even younger and more slender man in a grey tunic entered with a smile and a bow.

"What can I do for you?" he asked in Russian, the language in which the entire conversation was conducted.

"I want to visit China as a tourist, to stay about a month, to see whatever cities the Chinese tourist agency includes in its tours."

"Who are you?" he asked.

"An American student at MGU."

"Under whose auspices are you studying?"

"On the Soviet-American exchange program," I answered knowing full well the Chinese charge that Russians and Americans are plotting against them.

"I see," he said placidly. "Tell me more."

"I want to visit China to see a different society. I realize that relations between our countries are strained, but part of the trouble is that we don't know each other well. I want to understand China better."

He listened politely and even nodded agreement.

"What do you study in America?" he inquired, smiling.

"Political science."

"That's interesting."

Was it? I asked directly whether I could get a visa to visit China.

"Well, it would be very difficult." He smiled. "You know your government is not our friend. It hopes to destroy us and is attacking our allies in North Vietnam. It is not a good time to visit China. The Chinese people are angry with your government."

"I don't represent the government. I am a student and want to go as an ordinary tourist."

"Very difficult."

"Would you accept my application for a visa?"

"Very difficult."

He never ceased to smile and never said No. The word seemed to embarrass him. He preferred to talk about the room's Chinese furniture. He extracted a vase from the cabinet to show me the exquisite workmanship. He asked how old I was, congratulated me that I was in my twenties, and confessed with a grin that he was only thirty-two. He kept coming back to American foreign policy, but he didn't attack me; he seemed more grieved than angry.

After forty minutes of conversation I concluded there would be no visa and got up to go. But he had a request: Would I leave my name? When I hesitated, he hastily added, "You don't have to give it." I said I had no objection, and I carefully wrote it in Russian orthography on a blank page in a little black book that he handed me. I hope it didn't compromise either of us.

On the street outside, a few strollers watched me intently as I left the Embassy grounds, received the sentries' salute and walked toward the bus stop. A freezing wind had sprung up, but four men lounged on the corner, and a car waited down the road. I had little doubt about their identity, but I wasn't sure which bus to take, and they were the only people on the street. I asked one for directions, and he was helpful. I didn't see these men again. There were no repercussions from the Soviet authorities.

With China not unexpectedly out of the picture, I decided to visit East Europe on my way home. After nine Moscow months, Bucharest, Sofia, Belgrade, Budapest, and Prague were refreshingly relaxed and almost Western in spirit. The contrasts were striking. There were more cars in East European capitals and many more foreign cars; in Bucharest the taxis were Soviet-made Volgas, but many private autos were Fiats. Food in restaurants was better and served faster, and everywhere there were convenient self-service cafeterias of the kind Moscow badly needs. There were more Western-made goods in stores, and lines of customers were shorter. Window displays were more artfully arranged, particularly in the small privately owned shops in Belgrade and Budapest. In Belgrade I could buy *The New York Times, Time Maga-*

zine, and the *London Times* at newsstands. In Budapest I got *The New York Times* at the porter's desk of a hotel. When I asked a hotel porter in Prague, he looked guilty and said, "We don't sell *The Times.* We're not as advanced as the Hungarians."

One of Belgrade's papers is a tabloid complete with centerpiece pictures of Beatles and girls in bikinis, and with comic strips starring the Cisco Kid and what I hope wasn't their notion of modern America, Mutt and Jeff. Moscow goes in for Western movies, but Belgrade is not afraid of westerns like *Cat Ballou* and *How the West Was Won,* war pictures like *The Guns of Navarone,* and light ones like the Doris Day—Rock Hudson films. On the bank of the Sava River there is a museum devoted to the kind of contemporary art not visible in Moscow, and Bucharest's modern collection is not too far behind. Prague shows its tolerance of avant-garde notions, perhaps to its chagrin, in a host of young men wearing their hair at shoulder length.

In Bucharest, Sofia, and Budapest I was surprised and delighted when the National Tourist Offices suggested I stay in private homes, an idea unheard of in the Soviet Union. I was even more astonished in Belgrade when I was left free to find a place for myself. I had been dreaming of freedom, but it was raining as I tramped the streets searching for a hotel, and I almost wished I were back in the arms of a paternalistic state tourist agency. In Prague, where I was also left to my own devices, I landed a low-priced room at Charles University.

Nowhere in East Europe was I aware of police surveillance. My only concern was an excess of hospitality. I got more invitations than I could accept to visit people in their homes, to dine out with them, or to see the sights with them. I heard more honest, frank talk than I could remember, and I got on to controversial topics faster than I ever did in the Soviet Union. East Europeans asked relatively few questions about the U.S.A.; they seemed to be very well-informed about us. They preferred to make clear to an American the differences between their countries and the U.S.S.R.

A Rumanian airline clerk noticed that my baggage had been tagged in Moscow. "The Russians are uncivilized," she commiserated, "but now you're in Europe."

When I attempted to speak Russian instead of French to Rumanian students, they said, No, thank you. Russian was a *"langue brutale,"* and they would just as soon forget what they had learned of it in school. When I left Bucharest, my student friends gave me a souvenir post card, not a picture of Lenin or even Rumanian Party leader Nicolae Ceausescu, but a pinup snapshot of Italian film star Claudia Cardinale.

"The long lines in Moscow are intolerable," a Yugoslav student told me. I agreed; but when I tried to talk about the historical reasons for the queues and to sympathize with Russians who had to stand in them, he cut me off. "Don't worry about the Russians. They like to stand in lines."

When I talked Russian in Belgrade, I got dirty looks from Yugoslavs. Only one group was genuinely pleased to hear Russian. A band of Soviet tourists asked me how to get to the Modern Art Museum and when I told them, they congratulated me: "How well you Yugoslavs speak Russian!"

When I spoke Russian in Budapest, the looks I got were even more hostile. Some Hungarians I met forbade me to speak it in their presence. And even those who defended Hungary's friendship with the Soviet Union did so with reservations. A ranking Party intellectual justified Soviet intervention in 1956 and then hastened to put his pro-Soviet words in perspective.

"It was fortunate that they intervened because, whatever the motives of men like Imre Nagy, the old guard was returning. Cardinal Mindszenty was ready to give the land back to the landowners, and pogroms had begun against anyone linked with the Communists. Since 1956, the Russians have helped our economy by giving us long-term credit on very good terms. But that doesn't mean we particularly admire them or want to become like them. Their trial of Sinyavsky and Daniel was a fiasco, and it stirred up indignation. We are a small country, and we can't fight the Soviet Union."

I had assumed that Bulgarians and Czechs were the Soviet Union's most loyal allies because their ties were historical as well as ideological and because they had real affection for the Russians. Sofia's old monument to Tsar Alexander II testifies to the historical connection and, indeed, Bulgarians sounded off least against Moscow. But not so in Czechoslovakia.

"Who told you we are fond of the Russians?" demanded a Czech student. "It isn't true. We dislike them as much as anyone else does."

"We are *tovarishchi* until five o'clock and misters after that," a young engineer remarked coolly.

It was one thing to assure an American that East Europe was not the U.S.S.R. But what would East Europeans say about their own Communist Parties and systems? The criticism I heard was harsher than in the Soviet Union, and what there was of praise was faint. Most striking was the fearless, almost casual way people of all ages and stations blurted out the most unflattering judgments. Hungarian students declared, almost in passing, that Party members were careerists and opportunists. Less bitter, but no less emphatic, was a leading journalist who volunteered that he was not a Party member. "Most of my friends are not Communists either, yet we live well. We would have been Communists before the war when the Party was in opposition. But now that it's a ruling party, a man has more freedom out of it."

Hungarians complained bitterly about election slates with only one candidate. They flatly called such plebiscites a sham and were only mildly enthusiastic about a proposed system that would permit several condidates, all pledged to support the Party line.

"It's the best we can hope for under the circumstances," a lawyer remarked glumly, then brightened. "At least it's better than the Soviet elections. Our Parliament is not exactly the House of Commons, but at least our deputies can stand up to a government minister with hostile questions."

How does a young East European feel about compulsory service in his country's armed forces? Would he refuse to fight an unjust war? These questions, which are so agonizing to many young Americans, came up a number of times in Hungary and Czechoslovakia.

"For God's sake," said a Hungarian graduate student who was a Party member. "I bet almost every Russian would go to battle with spirit to defend Party and country. But a lot of Hungarians would not. Perhaps that reflects poorly on our system. But it speaks well of our youth."

Young Czechs reacted like the Hungarians. I met a young actor at a Prague theater. He had a Beatle coiffure, a gentle smile, and a date with the army in October.

"Of course I don't want to go," he said. "Only fools look forward to serving. Everybody knows that. But I can't afford an education, which would get me a deferment. The state gives stipends to good students. But if your parents have some money, they must pay. My father has enough to pay for my sister's education, but not for mine."

Czech students in Charles University were anxious to prove that they were under no ideological illusions. Like Soviet students they denounced their political and ideological courses as a bore, and some even dared to question the most basic Communist tenet, the nature of the Revolution.

"Our revolution in 1948 was not a People's Democratic Revolution," said a chap from the provinces who was in Prague on vacation. "It was a coup d'état. The Communists used the police and the threat of Soviet intervention to seize power."

That was a version I had heard in the United States, but I had not expected to hear it in Prague.

"Naturally they don't teach it that way." My friend sipped his beer in the dormitory snack bar and gazed at me shrewdly. "But we know."

"Your Averill Harriman once said an interesting thing," chimed in another Czech. "He said no Communist Party has ever come to power through open, honest elections. He was right."

Where had he heard about Averill Harriman's judgment? "We have a special eating club," he explained, confidentially, "where professors tell us a lot of things we can't read in the newspapers. They also express opinions they wouldn't mention in class."

The men and women at Charles University were an extroverted bunch. There were Hungarians, East Germans, and Poles, as well as Czechs. Like students everywhere, they fooled around, sang songs, philosophized, and argued. They had a rich gift for the good-humored insult. Czechs blasted the Hungarian national character, accusing Hungarians of descending in hordes on Prague to buy up sausage at low prices. Hungarians retorted that the Czechs were a mean and narrow race. In this company, the East Germans looked and sounded downright bourgeois. They came down to the snack bar every evening promptly at 11:00 to guzzle their beer, fondle their girls, and sing "Roll Out the Barrel" and another ditty called "Juanita Banana" which, as they performed it, went "Wa, wa, wa, wa, wa, wa, wa (breath), wa, wa, wa, wa, wa, wa, wa."

At one of these lively evenings in Prague, a Czech girl announced proudly that more and more of her contemporaries and teachers were returning to the Church.

"That's going too far," objected a Hungarian. "Just because you're alienated doesn't mean you have to become superstitious."

When I said I had seen more young people in churches in East Europe than in the Soviet Union, the Hungarian snorted, "Thank God for the Soviet Union. That sounds like the only consistent place left in the world. In the West, capitalism turns young people into socialists, and in the East socialism drives them to church."

I rented a car in Prague and drove west-northwest, stopping for a few days in Cheb, several kilometers from the West German border. Although Cheb looked like a sleepy little town, it was full of life and curiosity. Its theater had an active repertory, including Arthur Miller's *Death of a Salesman,* Tennessee Williams' *Orpheus Descending,* and Frank Gilroy's *Who'll Save the Plowboy?* A staff member almost apologized for the lack of avant-garde plays. "It's not a question of political censorship. It's a matter of public taste. We bus in workers and peasants from all over the provinces and they prefer uncomplicated entertainment. So we leave Ionesco and Pinter to Prague."

I met a young painter in Cheb who was also defensive. He said he would give almost anything to travel to Paris or New York, but the government would not permit Czechs to travel freely. It was not likely, he added resignedly, that these restrictions would soon be abolished.

"Aren't you a pessimist?" I asked.

"No, a realist."

In East Europe, as in the Soviet Union, the right to travel freely was a key issue. Hungarians, who had achieved a measure of such freedom, spoke condescendingly of Soviet barriers. Any Hungarian with money, I was told, could get up and go, at least within the Eastern Bloc and, within limits, to the West. Yugoslavs crowed that they could go as far as funds allowed.

Yugoslavs made a frequent point of the freedom their artists and writers had to create without state interference. They mentioned the wide variety of Western works on display in the country. They ridiculed socialist realism as a theory. Ideally, they said, the only requirement should be talent, but they admitted that occasionally favoritism and envy had served as criteria for dispensing state subsidies. What about Mihajlo Mihajlov? A regrettable exception, they replied, but the trouble was not socialist realism but his effort to push too far, too fast.

I happened to be in Belgrade when Tito purged Vice-President Alexander Rankovic and reduced the powers of the secret police. Yugoslavs didn't even try to conceal their delight from a foreigner.

"That was Tito's last and greatest gift to the Yugoslav people," said a student at a jazz jam session at Belgrade University. "They've talked about democracy and decentralization, but until now it was the police, not the people, who have been gaining new powers."

Virtually every East European I met coupled a distaste for the Soviet Union with a wish for improved relations with the West, particularly with the United States.

"We need better relations with you," said a Czech student. "We want to trade with you and to exchange the fruits of our cultures."

A simple solution; but the problem, to the best informed and most subtle minds, was much more complex.

"The trouble in East Europe," a distinguished Hungarian intellectual told me reflectively, "is that we have too many conflicting loyalties. There is Communism. There is the Church. There is the memory of closer ties to the West. Most important, there is a deep reservoir of national identity and pride. Russians may grumble about Communism, but at least it's their own. They made their own Revolution and their own mistakes. That's why they can laugh at themselves. But in East Europe it's not so easy. It was not everybody's revolution. Soviet power helped to make it, and then abused it. In many ways the most popular thing a Communist Party can do is to come out against Moscow. That's why intellectuals, especially non-Party people, are thinking about Switzerland and Sweden. Perhaps it's too late to follow their example, but the people are wondering what would have happened if we had followed another path."

It gradually dawned on me that the great East European irony was the widespread admiration everywhere for the United States, even though for years America had been officially condemned. Our movies, our plays, our jazz, our styles, our Coca-Cola, and much more important, our technology were being adopted. Even if Party and Government leaders wanted to, they could no longer, it seemed to me, stem the tide of American influence, which was rising faster in East Europe than in the Soviet Union.

20

"Tell It Like It Is"

SOME MONTHS after I returned from the Soviet Union, I attended a lecture at Columbia University by Anatoli A. Gromyko, the son of the Soviet foreign minister. An important man in his own right, the younger Gromyko directs the African Institute of the Soviet Academy of Science. His topic was "The Soviet Union Today," and in the audience were faculty members and graduate students specializing in Soviet affairs. Speaking excellent English, he dispensed sanctified Communist doctrine with the humorless air of a man who was utterly unaware that his sophisticated audience had heard and read it hundreds of times before: Marxism was scientific socialism; the brilliant leader of the Bolsheviks had been a man called Lenin; the Soviet Union was building Communism, and in all likelihood, the present generation would live under Communism. The audience, out of politeness, refrained from laughter. I could only think that if he had delivered this address to MGU students they would have been a lot less well-mannered.

Soviet leaders, I am convinced, have misunderstood and underestimated the mood and potential of the new Soviet generation, just as we in the United States have. They, I think, have been taken in by their own propaganda. We have been misled by their propaganda and our own. We both are in grave danger of miscalculating the influence of young Soviets on the future of their own society and its relations with the rest of the world. Both of us would do well to look objectively at these young people who will shape the Soviet future and with whom we will have an urgent need to communicate.

I speak of a key segment of Soviet youth, of men and women who are already an elite, who represent the brightest hopes of their country in the fields they study at MGU. No one can predict who will reach the top in the Soviet system, but I have no doubt that among the country's leaders will be talented and ambitious persons emerging from an ambience like that of MGU.

The Communist Party and Komsomol leadership have, it seems to me, underestimated the extent of disaffection and misjudged the sources of discontent. Leonid Brezhnev believes that an insignificant minority of youth is disaffected and that an overwhelming majority is actively committed to Party policies. Speaking at a plenary session of the Komsomol Central Committee on February 1, 1967, he said:

> It would be an unforgivable mistake not to notice that there are some young people, however insignificant their number, who, lacking experience in life and sufficient theoretical training, manifest a political looseness, an unconcern, and, I would say, a devil-may-care attitude toward life. This is unacceptable. It is not enough today to be satisfied that the absolute majority of Soviet youth fulfill their civic duty with high responsibility, profoundly understanding and actively carrying out the policies of the Party. Our task is to struggle for the mind of every young person, to see to it that every one is convinced and every one takes an active position in life . . . to bring up steadfast, ideologically committed fighters, dedicated to the end to the great goal of building Communism.

Let's assume that the disaffected are only an insignificant minority. If so, they get a lot of attention from the highest Party authorities, who are constantly analyzing the causes of the difficulty. According to Party analysts, the sources of the trouble are threefold:

(1) The corrupting influence of Western books, movies, plays, radio broadcasts, and even tourists. At the Twenty-third Party Congress, Komsomol leader Pavlov warned that "imperialism has been organizing ideological diversions . . . trying to introduce ideological infections into socialist society, bombarding the souls of the Soviet people with lies, slanders and misinformation." He declared that Soviet youth has "a strong constitution, a good immunity," but he had to report that at times young people showed "a weak knowledge of the laws of social development."

(2) The influence of Soviet artists and writers who, instead of preaching the Party's positive message, turn apolitical, or stress "shortcomings" of the Soviet past and present. At the Twenty-third Congress Moldavian Party leader Ivan I. Boldiul accused Tvardovsky, Solzhenitsin, and others of "producing pessimism, skepticism and decadence [by] tendentiously distorting certain epochs of the life of the Soviet people." Brezhnev seemed to take a more slightly moderate line, welcoming constructive criticism, which "helps Soviet people to overcome their shortcomings." But Pavlov lashed out at artists and writers who set a bad example for youth when they "substitute poses for positions, carping for passion, meditation for activity . . . [when they] accept the praises of the West . . . and . . . preen themselves with their ostentatious 'boldness,' with their principled 'apoliticalness.' "

(3) The failings of the Party's own theoreticians and propagandists who, according to fast-rising Moscow Party chief Nikolai G. Egorychev, are "lagging behind in . . . political economy, philosophy, scientific Communism . . . Party history . . . [thus] creating well-known difficulties in

the ideological upbringing of our youth, and producing, in certain politically untempered young people, an element of nihilism and skepticism."

Before looking more closely at these sources of disaffection, let me say a word about the contention that it is only a minority that is disaffected. Despite brave declarations, discontent at a place like MGU is more widespread and complicated than Party leaders realize or admit. The young people I encountered did not fit into easy categories of insignificant minority and overwhelming majority. Nearly all were both loyal and skeptical. Nearly all fulfilled their civic duty with responsibility, yet disagreed profoundly with many Party policies. Nearly all were dedicated to building the future, yet pessimistic about the prospects for achieving the Party's euphoric goals.

Nor do Party leaders adequately describe the source of skepticism. The cause is the Party's own rigidity and not the influence of the West or of the Soviet's own critical intellectuals. It is true that young Russians ask embarrassing questions. But that has been inevitable since contacts were widened with the West and since Khrushchev shattered the Stalin myth. It is too late to recapture lost innocence. The crucial test now is how Party leaders and theoreticians answer youth's questions, how they deal with the challenges of the West and with their own shortcomings. The inescapable truth is that young Russians are largely disenchanted with the Party's official answers. That is why they seek information directly from the West, and that is why they turn to the critical writers.

If young Soviets knew young America's battle cry, they would shout it to their own Party leaders: "Tell it like it is!" Like many young Americans, they are disturbed by the gap between reality and certain versions of it. They want to know the whole truth, for better or for worse, and they fear that for too long they have not had it. They are asking their leaders to level with them, whether the subject is Soviet past, present, or future, life in the West, China, or the prospects for radical change in underdeveloped areas.

Party spokesmen are distressed that young people are so concerned with the mistakes of the past. Young Russians reply that the Party line so accentuates the positive that anyone who examines the negative is only balancing the books. They feel that they are consistent when they defend their system's successes to an outsider and strike out at failures in sessions with Party speakers. They feel they are consistent when they demand to read for themselves the works of Stalin as well as such victims as Trotsky and Bukharin. They are aware that the ceaseless rewriting of history has obscured the truth, and they eagerly reach out for what rings true, whether in the frank memoirs of a general who was there or in an honest novel by a forthright writer. Having reached maturity after 1953, they see clearly that the men who later debunked Stalin were his collaborators and that among those who rule the country today are men who rose in the ranks when Stalinism was at its worst. Yet they do not reject Stalin's successors; as realists, they ask themselves whether it was possible to oppose Stalin and continue to function.

When a Party speaker complained at an MGU Komsomol briefing that young people were fascinated by present shortcomings, a student shot back that "things are so good, according to the Party, that it's the shortcomings that stand out." Party theoreticians have only themselves to blame if students do not flock to lectures on scientific Communism and Party history as enthusiastically as they go to courses where teachers offer a minimum of political and ideological pap. It is no accident, to use a phrase favored by Party leaders, that natural sciences are most popular at MGU or that a new field like sociology is attracting so many adherents. Party leaders themselves evoke the warmest response from young Russians when they are most candid. Thus Kosygin is particularly respected and so are the economic reforms that he introduced. In admitting that the economy needed decentralization, that something had to be done to improve the quality of goods, and that men are motivated by desire for profits, he "told it like it is." By the same token, Party leaders evoke the deepest cynicism when they are not frank, when, for example, they blame crime in the Soviet Union on bourgeois remnants and when, by default, they let Western radio bring first reports of bad tidings.

And the same goes for the future. Young Russians want planners to level with them. They prefer Kosygin's cautious predictions to Khrushchev's braggadocio. They are ready to build the future but resent being conned with fanfare of trumpets.

It is ironic that many young realists adopt a different standard toward the masses, for whom, they think, propaganda fanfares may be necessary. The very students who want to know the whole truth about the West are capable of arguing that more impressionable compatriots are not to be trusted. As for themselves, they want more Western books, newspapers, films, and all sorts of contact, whether their own travel to the West or Westerners to the Soviet Union. They are impatient with restrictions. Take the case of the MGU professor, an expert on America, who wanted to borrow my copies of *The New York Times.* He could read *The Times* in the Lenin Library or at the Institute of International Relations, but it was more convenient to borrow mine. Yet he was afraid to ask me. He arranged to have a Soviet student borrow the papers, wrap them in brown paper, and bring them to him. I am sure that the professor and his accomplice were ashamed. Surely they knew that the editors of *Pravda* have their copies of *The Times* and regarded themselves as no less trustworthy.

Young Russians want to learn from the West, particularly

the United States. The pother about their interest in jazz, jeans, and chewing gum has obscured the more significant fact that serious students want most the lessons of technology and industry that can help improve the fabric of Soviet life. The purchase of a Fiat automotive industry from Italy was perhaps the most popular move by the Soviet government in some time. And young Soviets want to go further, to import more consumers goods and the secrets of marketing and packaging which could shorten the long lines for goods and services. They have no patience with a bureaucrat who cannot figure out how to dry clean suits with buttons on, while he fulminates against the decadence of those who can. They are fascinated by the theory, attacked in the Soviet press, that all industrial societies have common problems of modernization, technology and management, the solutions to which have little to do with ideology. They even have the impression that Russians and Americans resemble each other, that we are both informal, outgoing, generous, and broadly good-humored; that both of us lack the discipline of the Germans, the style and sophistication of the French, the cool reserve of the English, and the touchy national pride of East Europeans. They believe that we are big enough to be capable of great good if we cooperate, or unimaginable harm if we clash.

Young Russians are not anti-capitalist in the way many Americans are anti-Communist. They do not feel menaced by capitalism or capitalist states; they are not interested in any anti-capitalist crusade or in a war to make the world safe for Communism. No doubt there are Party leaders who lament youth's lack of vigilance. But actually young Russians are more in tune with Party leaders on the issue of war than on any other. Youth is patriotic and if called to battle, even against the United States, would go—not with bravado, for they share their fathers' abhorrence of war, but with resolution. They believe in peaceful coexistence and defend it against those in East and West who pay only lip service to it.

They cannot understand how Americans can tolerate an anti-Communist crusade or burn and kill to save Vietnam from Communism. In doing so, they contend, America is risking all in the name of ideology, thus violating the very principles which they admire most. Young Russians are quick to resent an authority like the Colonel General who, in an MGU lecture, assured them that the socialist system would win any nuclear war. When he invited written questions from the floor, ten of the first fifteen demanded to know, "How can anyone win a nuclear war?"

On China, Party leaders and youth are in accord, perhaps because Soviet policy has been restrained. I have no doubt that Chinese are more acceptable than Americans as objects of antagonism; it is easier to get mad at yellow people who demand sacrifices than at rich white Americans who propose that Soviet people imitate their affluence. Yet on China, too, youth is challenging the highest authorities to be more objective, to explain the origin of Maoism. So far Party spokesmen have replied that Mao, like Stalin, is an aberration. When a student I knew reported quite objectively on the roots of Maoism to a Party history seminar, he was accused by his professor of "trying to justify the anti-Soviet policy of the Maoist clique."

When Party propaganda raves about national liberation movements in underdeveloped lands, youth provides a sober corrective, pointing out that these admirable causes can get terrible chaotic and distorted—witness the Congo. When Party leaders hail Outer Mongolia for building socialism, young Russians remark laughingly that the socialist structure in Mongolia is flimsy. But to sober analysts these young people pay close attention.

"We are living in a complex and often bewildering world, *tovarishchi*," said such a Party lecturer to a rapt MGU gathering one evening. "How shall we explain the military coups in Nigeria and Ghana? There's no clear or simple answer. In

Algeria they ousted Ben Bella and yet retain his foreign policy. They suppressed the Communist Party in Indonesia without changing foreign policy radically. It's all very complex."

When Party leaders sound off about Soviet youth, the young need only look in the mirror to check the description. They know that their motives and feelings are mixed. They are fully aware that they must make do without the comforts and luxuries that Americans take for granted, an acceptance of reality regarded by the Party as admirable. But they do not conceal their desire to have those comforts as soon as possible and this, according to the Party line, is not so admirable. Their naturalness about dating and sex makes American college weekends look like feverish tribal rites and is far in advance of the moralistic professions of Party pronouncements. If God is dead, as Party dogma insists and most students agree, ideology also is dying, and personal ethics can manage nicely without either.

How have we in the United States gone wrong in our conception of Soviet youth? We too have underestimated the extent of dissent and misjudged its significance.

We are right when we talk about a minority of alienated who retreat into apolitical silence, since the kind of uncompromising dissent they would utter would be considered treason. Organized opposition is impossible. And as Sinyavsky and Daniel found out, conspicuous dissent is punished. If burning draft cards is illegal in the United States, it is inconceivable in the Soviet Union.

But we are wrong about the Komsomol activists and young Party members who form another minority at the opposite extreme. Party leaders hail them as an ideologically tempered vanguard. We, referring to them as fanatical, dogmatic, and vigilant, suspect that they are a rear guard, that they lack receptivity to new ideas and are looked down on by their fellows. Some, at a place like MGU, are indeed mediocrities.

Others are not fanatical or dogmatic or particularly vigilant, and if they are not necessarily a vanguard, neither do they trail behind. They have their doubts, too, often substantial ones. As I understand it, Party members are bound by Party rules to voice their dissent before decisions are taken at closed Party meetings. You would not expect them to challenge their Party superiors at open meetings or to express their misgivings to an American. Yet the surprising thing is that I heard them get up and talk back to Party officials at open meetings, and on a number of occasions they aired their grievances to me.

We have made our gravest error in evaluating the majority which, we say, includes people who accept the Party line passively, and those who, though they have some reservations, remain silent and appear to accept it. Why do so many Russians accept the line, whether actively or passively? We give great credit to the power of propaganda and indoctrination. We say that education at a place like MGU teaches the young to be experts in their fields, but not to challenge the philosophical assumptions behind what they learn. And to explain the silence of those with only partial reservations, we say that he who speaks out is punished. Some analysts go so far as to argue that the Soviet government, by discouraging dissent, cuts itself off from knowledge about how its people think and feel.

But we are wrong about those in the middle. They do not necessarily accept the Party line, even passively; and they are not always silent. They can and do speak out, expressing surprisingly fundamental dissent. Some go so far as to question the merits of a one-party system. Some probe the historical significance of Trotsky and Bukharin. Some ponder the inevitability of Stalinism in a Communist system.

The simple truth is that Soviet indoctrination has backfired. It has ended in doubt and dissent. And Soviet education, perhaps in spite of itself, has produced a generation that questions all kinds of philosophical and political assumptions. We delude ourselves when we persist in the notion that this is a nation of sheep. We must recognize that the Party today does not equate all ideological nonconformity with criminal delinquency, that, far from penalizing outspoken students, it encourages them to be frank.

The meetings at MGU served as a kind of feedback mechanism. Again and again Party officials returned to MGU to debate all sorts of issues with the students. When a man as important as Peter N. Demichev, the Politburo's secretary in charge of ideological work, came to MGU to address 1,500 students in *Aktovyi Ẓal,* he became involved, I heard on good authority, in the kind of give and take that I witnessed at the meeting with the lecturer from the Central Committee.

There is much more dissent among Soviet youth than we have thought—and among their elders, too. Yet curiously the turmoil is, I think, a sign of Soviet progress and social health. My Soviet friends, dissenters themselves, thought so, too. They agreed with the man from the Central Committee that twenty years ago this kind of open debate would not have been possible. One friend told me that even five years ago he could not have talked to me as frankly as he did. If I am right that a prime source of discontent is the regime's unwillingness or inability to level with youth, then the growing public dialogue gives it the chance to get a better idea of what is on young peoples' minds. There are some Americans who say that this sort of sparring has been going on many years, but Soviet old-timers assure me that it is new.

If this is a new and vitally important trend, as I believe it is, how should we in the West take advantage of it to set up better lines of communication with Soviet youth? Since we begin with the great good will of young Russians, our best approach is to be ourselves. We will not impress them by broadcasting self-adulation, for that is what they have turned against at home. We will not win their admiration by belaboring their country's shortcomings, for that is the approach they disdain in Soviet propaganda about the United States. We will only antagonize them by exaggerating their disaffection and gloating over it; they remain socialists as well as patriots and are working in their own way to improve their society and the quality of their lives. We must hew to the truth; and the more honest we are about ourselves, the more they will respect us. Together the United States and the Soviet Union have the power to bring peace and abundance to the entire world. The hope of the future depends in no small measure on how we reach out to exchange ideas and ideals with the new Soviet generations.